KNIGHT WORK

Terance,

God Bless my friend.
Thank you for what you
do to make our world better.

Lloyd Knight

KNIGHT WORK

My Unfinished Journey of VETLANTA

LLOYD KNIGHT

XULON PRESS

Xulon Press
2301 Lucien Way #415
Maitland, FL 32751
407.339.4217
www.xulonpress.com

Paperback ISBN-13: 978-1-66287-446-8

Ebook ISBN-13: 978-1-66287-447-5

CONTENTS

1. Worst Day of My Life.................................1

2. Journey into the Military 7

3. Loadmaster Journey................................27

4. Journey to Adventure.............................37

5. Journey to Leadership 65

6. Civilian Transition Journey 77

7. Corporate America Journey 85

8. Changing the Culture Journey 107

9. Journey into VETLANTA 119

10. The VETLANTA Journey Continues................. 145

11. Faith Journey.....................................159

12. Till We Meet Again................................ 169

1
WORST DAY OF MY LIFE

I know for certain that we never lose the people
we love, even to death. They continue to partici-
pate in every act, thought, and decision we make.
Their love leaves an indelible imprint in our mem-
ories. We find comfort in knowing that our lives
have been enriched by having shared their love.
–Leo Buscaglia, Author & Motivational Speaker

Seplember 28, 2021, was the worst day of my life. I pray
that I'll never have to experience that type of intense pain
and anguish again. This was the day my high school sweetheart and bride of almost thirty-four years, Suzan Marie Knight,
passed away unexpectedly. She had become ill on the day
after we returned home from one of our amazing vacations
and died two days later from a rare bacterial infection. After
I made the decision to take her off life support and said my
goodbyes along with my two sons James and Brandon, I sat
alone in an empty waiting room completely devastated not
knowing what I was going to do in the next ten minutes, let
alone the next ten days, ten months, or ten years. This was the
tragedy of tragedies for our family as my love, my best friend,
the mother of our sons, and my biggest supporter was taken
without notice and gone forever. To be very honest, I wanted

to die with her at the hospital and would have been more than content if I'd been struck down by a car in the hospital parking lot while walking out.

My first action was to pray, and with prayer I made the decision in the waiting room that I needed to do everything in my power to see Suzan again and to continue to live so I could honor her, but I didn't know how to start. I didn't know if I had the strength to continue and I was lost like I've never been lost before. I kept thinking and repeating *What am I going to do?* as the helplessness overwhelmed me again. I was lost again, but within seconds, my phone started ringing. My VETLANTA family had heard the news and mobilized into action. Their friendship, love, and compassion would help me through the extremely dark days, weeks, and months which lay ahead.

In my fifty-three years, nothing had ever prepared me for the grief that I would experience. I was sad, angry, heartbroken, anxious, depressed, in shock, and I even became mad with the Air Force as for years they had taught us the textbook stages of grief. They never mentioned in these classes that the stages would sometimes happen in minutes. They never mentioned they don't happen in chronological order and that the grief would come and go constantly all day and night. There were so many emotions that I had to process and that I continue to work through, including guilt of her dying and me living.

Thank goodness, my VETLANTA family was there to help me work through these emotions. Thank you, John, Melissa, Kevin, Zack, Patrick, Amy, Krista, Tim, Matt, Roger, Chris, and Lisa, for those meals we shared, the tenderness you showed, the walks, the hours you listened, the hugs, the tissues, the laughs when I needed to smile, for relating the shared memories, and for steering me to Christ. Thank you to my current and former UPS coworkers who were there for me including

Jordan, Stella, Terry, Rich, Norris, and Adnan. Thank you to my family as I know you cared deeply for Suzan and miss her.

After I prayed, my next thought was to quit everything including VETLANTA. I did quit Leadership Forsyth, my county's eight-month leadership program. I sent the program manager a quick email saying that Suzan had passed away and requested immediate disenrollment. A couple of hours later, I came to the realization that Suzan would have been furious with me for quitting. She was always supportive of the decisions I made, but anytime I tried to quit something because she wasn't feeling well, I got both barrels. It was okay to change your mind, but using her as an excuse was not acceptable in her opinion. With this realization, I reenrolled in Leadership Forsyth, which ended up being a nice distraction once a month and I was thrilled when they invited me back the next year to be a class facilitator. I also decided to remain as the President of VETLANTA as my work was unfinished and my journey was not complete. I made a promise to myself that I would ensure VETLANTA would remain in place to support the next veteran or family member who is facing tragedy.

Suzan was a huge supporter of VETLANTA from the beginning. She began showing up at our first summits along with my administrative assistant, Stella, because we needed people to fill seats. Suzan immediately figured out that we were on to something special, and we had the potential of connecting a highly effective and influential network to help veterans and their families. She started attending most our events and served exceptionally well as the "First Lady of VETLANTA," which is the title former board member Krista deKryger anointed her.

Suzan's engagement was so important to me. As president of a large organization, you don't always get honest feedback, but Suzan would always provide frank feedback and

3

straightforward advice especially when she thought I could do better. Some of the more studious VETLANTA members figured out if they went to her and made it through her rigorous vetting process, they could get front of the line privileges to talk to me at a summit. Sometimes, to make this happen she would give me a gentle tap on the shoulder to make introductions and other times she would give me a big shove when I wasn't paying her the appropriate attention. I so miss those taps and shoves.

One of the greatest resources I had as leader of VETLANTA was Suzan's perspective. Often, we would drive separately to our quarterly summits, since I had to be there early and stay late; but I would always call her on my way home. During these calls, she would tell me what went well, what didn't, who impressed her and who didn't. Her perspective was often the same as mine but sometimes it was very different; however, I always trusted her opinion, counsel, and advice.

Sometimes, we would be able to ride to the summits together and on more than one occasion, on our way back to the office to pick up my car, we became so engaged in our conversation that we got all the way home before we realized that my car was still at the office. The ride home after the first two summits without her was like getting hit in the gut from Iron Mike Tyson and Brock Lesnar at the same time. I didn't say it to you enough, Suzan, thank you for being my biggest fan and supporter. You were the best friend a man could ever have, the smartest and wisest partner and counselor anyone could ever ask for, you loved our sons unconditionally and you were by my side faithfully for almost thirty-five years. I miss and love you.

Suzan while on vacation in Bavaria in 2019

The reality is that you will grieve forever. You will not "get over" the loss of a loved one; you will learn to live with it. You will heal and you will rebuild yourself around the loss you have suffered. You will be whole again, but you will never be the same. Nor should you be the same nor would you want to. –Elisabeth Kubler-Ross and David Kessler, authors of *Five Stages of Grief*

2
JOURNEY INTO THE MILITARY

Who kept the faith and fought the fight; the glory theirs, the duty ours. –Wallace Bruce, Author, Poet, and Orator

My life has been an amazing journey and, even with the tragedy of Suzan's death, I'm aware that I 've had so many blessings over the years. If you know me personally, you've probably heard me refer to myself as Forest Gump because of all the interesting adventures I've had. Like Forest, I married my high school sweetheart, and my adventures include logging over 2,500 flight hours, traveling to over seventy countries, attending President Obama's last State of the Union Address, visiting the George H.W. Bush aircraft carrier at sea, meeting my favorite NASCAR driver during a tour of the Pentagon, attending an event at the White House, and presenting to Governor Brian Kemp to name a few. I could use the next line comparing my life to a box of chocolates, but my love of Forest Gump only goes so far. These adventures have become a part of my journey to VETLANTA and my desire to serve veterans and their families.

Suzan and I attending an Army National Guard VIP event at the Pentagon and spending time with the troops on a landing craft on the Potomac River in 2014

Meeting with Navy veteran, Congressman Andrew Clyde in 2022

Suzan and I attending an event in Washington DC in 2018

Left to Right, Major General Thomas Carden, Steve Cannon, Governor
Brian Kemp, First Lady of Georgia Marty Kemp, First Lady of VETLANTA
Suzan Knight giving me some love after my opening comments during a
VETLANTA Summit at Mercedes Benz Stadium in 2019.

Suzan and I flying in a Georgia National Guard Blackhawk in 2019

Suzan and I attending Army-Navy Football Game in Baltimore in 2014

Suzan and I on the field at Mercedes Benz Stadium prior to an Atlanta Falcons game in 2018

Suzan and I attending the Freedom Ball at the Georgia Aquarium in Atlanta

I always wanted to write a book and it's been one of the remaining items on my bucket list for several years, but I never thought I had a good enough story to hold readers' attention for an entire book. Not long ago, in just one week, I had three friends who are not connected tell me that I had a terrific story to tell and I needed to share it by writing a book, which I saw as a sign from God and decided to listen.

The purpose of this book is multi-fold. The first is to tell the VETLANTA story and provide best-practices and lessons learned to inspire other people and cities to create similar programs or organizations to help veterans and their families. Second is to share how faith and trust in God helped me through my loss. Third is to highlight some of the amazing organizations that support veterans. Fourth is to pass on leadership gems that I've learned along the way. Fifth is to provide humor, and I hope some of my stories will make you laugh because laughter and humor are so important to our wellbeing and have been a big part of my life. Finally, writing this book is part of my healing process. I've heard good things about journaling, but I personally never thought it would be beneficial to me. But after writing just the first five pages, I get it. My initial plan for this book was to not make it about me, however the story of VETLANTA needs context and the journey to VETLANTA is my story.

I was born into a military family. My dad is an Army veteran who retired as a Sergeant First Class, working most of his career in food service. He grew up extremely poor with his parents and two brothers working as sharecroppers in Russellville, Kentucky, living in a house without running water or plumbing before they migrated to California to work as fruit pickers. He dropped out of high school to go to work delivering water and eventually joined the Army where he met my mother and my four future siblings. My mom is a feisty German and proud American Citizen born in Nazi Germany. She is from a very lovely village in the Nahe wine region called Bad Kreuznach. Like my dad, she also had a very tough childhood including spending countless hours in bomb shelters and having a home destroyed by American bomber planes. She ended up marrying the wrong person and lived in poverty in Michigan, Washington, and Idaho for many years before divorcing and meeting my dad.

I would come along the next year and was born in 1969 at Fort Benning, Georgia. We spent many years of my childhood living in Germany and lived at Fort Sill, Oklahoma. My dad retired at Fort Knox, Kentucky, where I had the rare opportunity for an Army brat to spend grades 8-12 in one spot. My brother Ed joined the Army and left home when I was in first grade. My sisters, Carol and Joann, totally spoiled me during my early years and left home when I was in middle school and my brother John spent the next several years kicking my butt in a successful effort to toughen me up.

My family's military history is substantial and includes my brother Ed, John who retired from the Air Force as a Senior Master Sergeant, two brothers-in-law who served in the Army, a niece who served in the Air National Guard and her husband who is a post 9/11 Army combat veteran, and my sister Joann who has worked for three plus decades as a civilian on Fort Knox. My oldest son James also joined the Army as a paratrooper in the 82nd Airborne and completed two combat tours in Afghanistan.

A proud mama with James during a graduation ceremony at Fort Benning

Suzan's family also included significant military service including her grandfather who was a highly decorated Army solider receiving two purple hearts in World War II. Her father and I use that term lightly as he didn't deserve the amazing daughters he had, or the father, he title also retired from the Army. Suzan's mother died from Leukemia at the age of twenty-three when Suzan was just three years old. Her dad was a bad man; however, her grandfather on the other hand was amazing and she was the apple of his eye. When I proposed to Suzan, she accepted my proposal but told me that we wouldn't be able to get married until I obtained his approval. I was blessed because not only did I get his approval, but we also bonded and developed a solid mutual respect of one another.

I never thought I would join the military growing up as I was primarily exposed to the Army, and I knew the Army lifestyle wasn't for me. I really liked airplanes growing up, loved to read stories about Chuck Yeager, and admired the Air Force, but I didn't believe I was smart enough to be a pilot as I was a terrible student from early on all the way through high school. I blamed my academic shortfalls on my overindulgence of sports and girls, which was partially true. I was an average but spirited athlete since I was in third grade and highly involved in sports throughout my early years. I enjoyed but wasn't very good at baseball and gave it up in the eighth grade and I gave up football in the tenth grade as my coaches were not interested in a 138-pound center or defensive end. I started wrestling in the eighth grade and wrestled varsity from ninth through eleventh grade and made the state finals in my final year where I lost both matches but was not pinned.

Wrestling provided a great foundation that would serve me well in years to come. It is an amazing sport which breeds positive character traits including mental toughness, commitment, discipline, honor, perseverance, responsibility, and sacrifice. It's a complex sport where humbleness and confidence go hand in hand with having a caveman mentality while being an expert in strategy and anatomy. I ended up giving up wrestling during my senior year as I was tired of cutting weight and wanted to have more fun. I ended up meeting Suzan and she would indeed be much more enjoyable than wrestling.

While I blamed my lack of academic success on girls and sports, the truth is, I really didn't have any discipline when it came to academics, so I never developed effective study habits. Lucky for me, I met this feisty, smart brunette during my senior year of high school who I fell madly in love with, and she helped me get my grades up to C's and D's. I would have never passed Humanities if it weren't for Suzan, and I didn't have the room to flunk any course. My parents wanted me to go to college and were going to pay for it, but I knew it would be a bad investment as I didn't have the discipline or determination to be successful in college at that time.

My best friend, David, decided to join the Kentucky Air National Guard in December of my senior year in high school and I decided to enlist with him. I'd volunteered to join the military for many reasons. The first was I needed a job. The national guard pay of $125 a month was attractive to me as there were few jobs in Hardin County, Kentucky, at that time and the only job I was able to land was at Murphy's Mart, which paid just $3.35 an hour and I was laid off three months after I was hired. I'm also patriotic and feel strongly about military service, so it was a natural fit. I wanted to be an Air Traffic Controller but the waiting list for that career field was almost two years long, so I chose the only available choice that kept me near airplanes and that was as a plane mechanic. The crazy thing is I'm about as far away from being mechanically inclined as you can get and still haven't completely figured out that whole *righty-tighty* and *lefty-loosey* puzzle.

Thankfully, my experience with the Kentucky Air National Guard helped me quickly figure out that I needed to look at other career field options. In 1986, the guard had this initiative called the Student Flight Program. This program allowed high school seniors who enlisted in the national guard to start their career immediately after enlisting and prior to attending basic training and tech school. The student flight program is designed to help new, non-prior service enlistees become better prepared for basic training, making the transition from civilians into military service easier. Before I knew it, I was issued fatigues and was trained and working on actual RF-4C Phantom aircraft.

The F-4 Phantom was a two-seat, twin-engine tactical fighter designed to cover the entire tactical mission, close air support, interdiction, and air superiority. It's a large and impressive fighter aircraft that was fully capable of effectively performing many missions over many decades and is still being used today by foreign militaries including, Greece, Turkey, Iran, and South Korea. The program was developed in 1953 by McDonnell Aircraft Corporation for the U.S. Navy and by the early 1960s, the U.S. Air Force recognized a new requirement which could be filled by the F-4 and an amazing 5,195 Phantoms were built.

In April 2007, just four months after enlisting in the guard, I proposed to Suzan, and she said yes. There was no way we were going to be able to make it on a traditional national guard salary, so I decided to change over to active duty. My guard unit was not thrilled with my decision since they had invested so much time and effort on me and my training, but to their credit, they helped me through the process. David remained in the Kentucky Air National Guard but converted to active duty Air Force shortly before Desert Storm when his guard unit switched from F-4 Phantom jets to C-130 Hercules cargo aircraft. He left the Air Force shortly after the war. My next step was to visit the active-duty Air Force recruiter in Elizabethtown, Kentucky, and the sergeant immediately did what most recruiters do to fill quotas and he pitched me a hardcore recruiting effort and highly encouraged me to enlist under the "open general" program.

If you aren't knowledgeable of the "open general" program it is a program where you agree to enlist, and the Air Force will decide what your career field will be after you enlist, during basic military training based on the needs of the Air Force at that exact moment in time. You agree to join without knowing what you are going to do. It's kind of like spinning the roulette wheel as you could end up with a very good match or you could end up doing something you would never want to do. No disrespect to any of my fellow airmen but that's a path to find yourself counting rivets of an aircraft while guarding it during winters at Minot

AFB, North Dakota, or to find yourself handing out basketballs at a gym in Thule, Greenland. I was enlisting not only to find employment, but I saw this as an opportunity for a career and wanted something which I believed I would be happy doing for many years.

The surprising thing is, although I was a terrible student in high school, I did extremely well on the Armed Services Vocational Aptitude Battery commonly referred to as the ASVAB. The ASVAB test is a multiple-aptitude battery that measures developed abilities and helps predict future academic and occupational success in the military. It is administered annually to more than one million military applicants, high school, and post-secondary students. *Future academic success?* Yeah right, after all this was me and future academic success was probably not in my cards if you based it off my academic records for my first thirteen years of school.

Since I was qualified per the ASVAB for almost every career field, I very confidently played my hand—which was a largely a bluff—and informed the recruiter that I was more than happy to stay in the Kentucky Air National Guard and would be back in twenty-four hours and if he didn't have some top-notch career field options, I would stay in the guard. To his credit, he listened and had five amazing options waiting for me when I came back. They included my future career field, Aircraft Loadmaster, as well as Boom Operator, Weather Specialist, Intelligence Specialist, and Armed Forced Network (AFN) Specialist. I'd like to believe I was cool enough to become an AFN radio or television reporter, but the fact of the matter was I was not very good with public speaking at that time and was still very shy around people who didn't know me. I quickly read the one-page overviews and decided to become an Aircraft Loadmaster. But to tell you the truth, I really didn't know anything about what the job entailed. I knew it was flying, I knew I would be able to see the world and they were even going to pay me an extra $125 per month for enlisted flight pay.

Five days after high school graduation, I said goodbye to Suzan and my parents and hopped on a Greyhound bus in Elizabethtown that took me to the Military Entrance Processing Station in Louisville where I endured another flight physical, completed the U.S. Military Oath of Enlistment, and hopped on a United flight for San Antonio, Texas, for Air Force Basic Military Training where I made it through without any issues. The Air Force has learned many lessons over the last several decades and has toughened up basic training some by adding more combat training to the curriculum, but I want to share details on my basic training experience so my Marine Corp and Army buddies can laugh at me even more than they already do. Many of the classes were military specific like learning how to march, Air Force history, first aid, how to wear the uniform, inspections and so forth but a large part of the curriculum was life skills like balancing your checkbook, creating a budget, signing a contract, learning about pay and allowances, and handling conflict. I only saw a firearm once during basic training where we shot a total of forty rounds on the M-16. My score on the rifle qualification course was zero as I ended up firing my rounds into the target next to mine, and that lucky Airman next to me earned a Marksman ribbon. Thankfully, there was not a pass or fail grade, but it gave my technical instructor plenty of ammo to make fun of me for my remaining days of basic training.

Our physical fitness regimen wasn't hard for me considering my wrestling background and it was even easier because outdoor exercise would be suspended during red flag conditions. A red flag is raised when the temperature reaches 88 degrees. Being that Air Force Basic Training is in San Antonio, Texas, and I went in June and July, the red flag was often up by the time we exited the dining facility for breakfast at 7:30 AM. I know my Marine and Army friends are laughing at all this including the terms, *dining facility*, *breakfast*, and *7:30 AM*. We did have the opportunity to complete this very cool obstacle course on the second to last day of basic training, but the Air Force brass ended up fluffing that up as well as between the obstacles, our technical instructors would yell at us to walk between events and slow down while completing the obstacles.

Everyone who made it to this point in basic training had technical school slots confirmed which would be starting the very next week and leadership didn't want any airmen getting hurt and not be able to start tech school. To make my Marine and Army buddies laugh even more, we had Saturday dances at the recreation center starting on week four and I saw Lou Rawls in concert on base during the Independence Day holiday. I can't say it was something that I would ever want to do it again, but it wasn't too challenging or stressful.

Basic Loadmaster School at Sheppard Air Force Base in Texas was a completely a different story. The course was extremely challenging with constant exams, lots of math, and tons of memorization. If you know me personally, you know I don't have the best memory in the world and in the Loadmaster career field a lot of information is required to be memorized, and I do mean a lot—ranging from math formulas to emergency procedures to how many gallons of waste the latrine holds. During the six-week tech school, over 50 percent of my fellow students flunked out of training including two friends I had made in my basic training. Flunking out of training would mean you could be released from your military service obligation, or you would have to go open general and be assigned a different career field.

I simply could not wash out as I didn't want to disappoint my parents and I had a fiancé at home counting on me. The bleak environment around me created self-discipline which I didn't know I had. I was able to dig in deep and persevere and these traits would serve me very well over the years. While I still didn't think I was very smart, I overcame this lack of confidence and ability with ferocious study habits. staying up past lights-out each night.

What I didn't realize at the time is studying was going to become a new way of life for me. I my twenty-year Air Force career I completed many schools and courses, including C-141 Loadmaster School, C-141 Loadmaster Airdrop School, C-5 Loadmaster School, C-23 Army Flight Engineer School, Academic Instructor School, Non-Commissioned Officer Preparatory School, Non-Commissioned Officer Academy, Senior Non-Commissioned Officer Academy, and the First Sergeant Academy. I also earned two associates degrees from the Community College of the Air Force and bachelor and master's degrees from American Military University and later a graduate certificate from the University of Georgia and even completed a UPS Global Perspectives Program at Emory University's Goizueta Business School. During the journey, I even managed to win academic awards including distinguished graduate, the commandant's award for leadership, honor graduate, dean's list, and president's list. My mom is still amazed and very proud of my academic accomplishments.

While I wasn't going to win any awards in tech school, I took my 75 percentile GPA and new enlisted aviation wings and headed to Air Force Survival School, which was located at Fairchild Air Force Base, Washington. Air Force Survival school is now known as Survival, Evasion, Resistance, and Escape School or SERE. The course lasts nineteen days and occurs forty-eight weeks out of each year with six days being spent seventy miles north of the base in the mountains of the Colville and Kaniksu National Forests. The course consists of physical and psychological stresses of survival, hands-on training in postejection procedures and parachute landing falls, survival medicine, and recovery device training and equipment procedures. In the field, students receive additional training which includes food procurement and preparation, day and night land navigation techniques, evasion travel and camouflage techniques, ground-to-air signals and aircraft vectoring procedures, and shelter construction. Finally, students are returned to Fairchild and receive Code of Conduct training in evasion and conduct after capture.

This was a challenging and exhausting course. The first three weeks consisted of classroom studies from 7:30 AM to 5:00 PM, and on most evenings we got together for group study or were assigned group projects that would often run past midnight. It was a very different environment for me as most of the class was comprised of officers and everyone was older than me by multiple years. The six days in the wilderness were equally exhausting but excellent. I was in very good shape, so I didn't mind the long hikes, but I stayed hungry. We were given one meals-ready-to-eat (MRE) per person, four survival bars—which have the taste, weight, and consistency of compacted saw dust—and one live rabbit per group of eight airmen. I lucked out with on the weather front once again as the lows were in the mid-40s and the highs in the 70s and it was a perfect time of year to complete this training. One of requirements of the class is to be able to start a fire in two minutes and it was super easy in the dry conditions of early fall. I felt bad for the airmen who must complete this course in the winter with fifteen feet of snow on the ground.

The core time in the wilderness consisted of instruction from the amazing SERE instructors who were like Eagle Scouts on steroids. There was a ton of hiking, rudimentary camping, amazing camaraderie, and lots of hunger. I was a growing teenager, so all the physical effort plus the little calorie intake made the course more challenging. The instructors did give us the opportunity to eat truly disgusting things to try to get us over food aversions. I say opportunity and that implies optional, but it wasn't. My first food aversion test was a worm. My instructor pulled out his fishing pole and had us dig in the ground for worms. Thinking I was going to have the opportunity to score trout or salmon, I found the biggest fattest worm I could, only to be ordered to eat it. While I'm a huge foodie and will eat almost anything put in front of me, this dish was not pleasant at all and almost made me hurl. I also had to eat ants, which strangely tasted like sweet tarts, and the coup de grace was eating the partially digested remains left in the rabbit's stomach, which my fellow airmen made me kill. My group, knowing that I was a city slicker and very young, picked me to kill the rabbit. They thought it would freak me out and I believe the instructor was a bit worried that the rabbit might suffer. They however underestimated my hunger and I hit that rabbit so hard with the thumping stick that I instantly became a legend and was serenaded to Elmer Fudd's "Kill the Rabbit" song for the rest of the course.

The final three days of land survival is something that just completely sucked and gave me the utmost respect for the prisoners of war who went through the real thing, especially for those who were captive for years. The Prisoner of War (POW) training and academic training immediately followed the time in the wilderness and was two days of classroom training followed by several days of being captive. It started off kind of lame as we were given a scenario and we boarded a bus for the ride over to the POW compound, but it got very real very fast. Our bus was attacked with flashbang grenades and gunfire (blanks) and several of the biggest and meanest looking dudes boarded the bus screaming at us while putting hoods over our heads.

The next several days consisted of sleep deprivation, more hunger, severe mind games, and even light physical torture. The highlights included being shoved naked into a cell which was slightly shorter than me, ordered to stay standing for hours on end, having cold water thrown on me throughout the night and listening to crazy Asian music, the phone ringing and a baby crying for hours. I was also shoved into a very small box which freaked me out at first but once I got the hood off, I figured out that it was warm, quiet and no one was throwing cold water on me, and I was able to get about an hour of sleep. When they opened the door of the box, I promptly fell out of it still sleeping and got a couple of kicks in the ribs for my disobedience.

After a day alone in isolation, we were put into a group camp and things mostly got better for everyone but me. Apparently, the strategy was to find the youngest person in the camp and designate them as the "war baby" and the camp guards would torture that person when one of us would be disobedient or screw up. The torture consisted of having a towel put around your neck and shaken which doesn't bad, but I can tell you that it really sucked. To make matters worse, the person who shook me was a female sergeant and she was part of the instructor cadre that road on the bus with the students back to the base and sat next to me. I was stunned, scared, and angry but I kept quiet for the entire trip back to the barracks. The POW camp experience ended on a highly patriotic note as my group was being pressured into saluting the flag of our made-up adversary. We rightly refused and after each time we faced an onslaught of screams and more skull rattling shakes. During the final attempt, we turned only to see "Old Glory" being raised and the National Anthem playing. I believe my heart was going to pound out of my chest but I was glad to have that experience past me. One thing I learned during this training was several top performers at the POW camp were female airmen. I was super impressed with their tenacity, strength, determination, resolve, and grace under pressure. Women at the time couldn't serve in combat but that would rightly change several years later. I also learned not to eat a large pizza from Dominos after you have only eaten a worm, ants, sawdust bars, and rabbit for a week.

In addition to land survival and the prisoner of war training, I completed water survival training which included lessons such as techniques in signaling rescue aircraft, hazardous aquatic life, food and water procurement, medical aspects of water survival, and life raft procedures. Water survival at the time was taught at the base swimming pool, which doesn't seem very challenging, but it was. For those movie buffs out there, it was very similar to the pool scenes in the movie *An Officer and a Gentlemen* and, lucky for me, we didn't have Lou Gossett Jr. as our instructor. I'm a big fan of the water and a decent swimmer so the course was not stressful, and I even had some fun during the training.

I was given one week of vacation and went home to Radcliff, Kentucky, where Suzan and I got married. The minister at our church required six weeks of pre-marital counseling but since we were in a military town and I was in the military, he waived the six-week requirement and decided he only needed to spend an hour with us. After just thirty minutes in his office, he became somewhat frustrated at our silliness and wrapped up the session early. We fared better with him than the county clerk when we went to pick up our marriage license. One of the questions on the form was "Are you related and if so, how?" I looked over at Suzan and said, "What do you think about this question, Sis?" and she replied back "Ya know, Ma doesn't like us talking about our relationship." The clerk was not amused and threw us out of her office, but not before giving us the license. We were married in a lovely ceremony where my family took care of everything and Suzan's grandfather drove all the way from Vian, Oklahoma, to give her away. My brother John did write "HELP ME" on the bottom of my shoes, which got a laugh from the crowd when we knelt in prayer. That night we stayed on the thirteenth floor at the Brown Hotel in Louisville and went to Chi Chi's Mexican restaurant and ordered milk for our drinks. The next day we went to the Louisville Zoo for our honeymoon and yes, we were such kids.

Suzan and I attending Air Force Association Conference in 1992

3
LOADMASTER JOURNEY

When once you have tasted flight, you will forever walk the earth with your eyes turned skyward, for there you have been, and there you will always long to return.–Leonardo DaVinci

My first assignment was with the Twentieth Military Airlift Squadron at Charleston Air Force Base, South Carolina. It was a great squadron with a long-storied history, and it was nicknamed the double X squadron because of the roman numerals on the patch and the going joke was we always had two strikes against us. Suzan's very first week as a military spouse gave her a real taste on what the life of an enlisted aviator was going to be like as we arrived on Sunday night, found an apartment on Monday, and I was sent to Germany on a four-day trip on Thursday. Suzan didn't even have a driver's license yet, but she was tough and independent and knew how to make things work.

I was at Charleston for about six weeks and was then sent to the six week long C-141B Loadmaster Qualification Training School at Altus Air Force Base, Oklahoma. If you have never been to Altus, Oklahoma, you are missing a garden spot of the country and, yes, this is sarcasm. Altus is approximately fifty miles west of Fort Sill and Lawton and is one of the few towns in the United States with a population that has shrank every census since 1980. It's a prairie town without much going on except for the base, which has been home to airlift training for many years and currently hosts training for C-17, KC-46, and KC-135 aircrews. Friday fun usually consisted of going to Sonic and Walmart and if studies were going well, we would head out to the North Mountain Wilderness Area and have a burger at Meers, which is hole in the wall joint that serves gigantic burgers served on pie tins. If you were there at the right time of the year you could attend the Mangum Rattlesnake Derby. Even better is the annual Holy City of the Wichita's Easter Passion Play, which is a narrated dramatization of the birth, life, death and resurrection of Jesus Christ. Promotional materials for the Passion Play proudly announce, "This Easter Passion Play is the longest running of its kind in the United States. Created in 1926, this passion play drama is held outdoors in the Holy City of the Wichita's near Lawton with the Wichita Mountains serving as a backdrop."

Flight school at Altus was as tough as initial Loadmaster Technical Training, but fewer airmen flunked out of this training because of the weeding out process in tech school. It was getting easier for me as I had developed solid study habits and became a disciplined student. It was a rigorous program with nine hours of class each day followed by two to four hours of individual and group study in the evenings. Even after graduating from this course, there would be another four weeks of classroom training when I returned to Charleston and four additional months of flying with instructors before I became a qualified C-141 Loadmaster able to fly without an instructor.

The C-141 Starlifter was the workhorse of Military Airlift Command for decades. It was built by Lockheed at their factory in Marietta, Georgia, and was the first all jet transport plane for the Air Force. President Kennedy opened the hangar doors remotely from the White House during the rollout in 1961 and the Starlifter made its first flight in 1963. A total of 285 Starlifters were built, and they remained in service for over forty years until the Air Force retired the last C-141 from service in 2006 and the aircraft was replaced by the C-17 Globemaster. The job of the Military Airlift Command was dangerous and a total of 19 Starlifters were lost due to accidents with dozens of personnel lost. All but 15 of the surviving aircraft have been chopped up and sold for scrap metal. The 15 remaining aircraft are on display at museums and Air Force bases across the country.

After I became qualified, I would primarily fly strategic airlift missions departing Charleston and resupplying military units throughout Europe flying each month to Germany, England, Italy, Spain, and the Azores with occasional trips to Panama, Puerto Rico, Kenya, Egypt, and Saudi Arabia. I also had a handful of very special trips. On one trip, which was highly classified at the time but has since been declassified, we carried six live dolphins from Mississippi to Hawaii. Dolphins have been trained to perform several tasks, including delivering equipment to underwater personnel, locating, and retrieving lost objects, and guarding boats and submarines. They have been trained to detect enemy swimmers, and this was the case in both the Vietnam war, as well as the Persian Gulf war.

The Loadmaster career field ended up being one of the most amazing careers that an eighteen-year-old without a college education could sign up for and is still a very relevant and important career in the Air Force today. Over the last thirty years, many aviation positions have been eliminated with technology advancements including navigators, radio operators, gunners, and flight engineers, but the Loadmaster career field is still going strong even on the newest aircraft. As a Loadmaster, one of the optional but nice things I used to do is bring coffee up to the crew on the fight deck after takeoff and I would always joke around with the Flight Engineers that I was doing that for job security. The going joke is being a Loadmaster is the best job in the world as we have college graduates fly us all around the world from one party to the next and honestly that wasn't too far from the truth in my first years of flying.

If you aren't familiar with what a loadmaster does, aircraft Loadmasters are responsible for supervising the loading and unloading of the aircraft, which includes pallets and vehicles loaded on the aircraft. A loadmaster's duties include mathematically preplanning the correct placement of the load on the airplane, providing passenger comfort and safety, securing cargo, and taking part in airdrop operations. Enlisted aviators in the Air Force are treated very well and because we were continually away from home, we weren't subject to many of the additional duties as other airmen. While we were generally treated very well the job can be very intense and stressful at times.

As a Loadmaster, I was responsible for the weight and balance of the aircraft and ensuring cargo is loaded and secured in a very specific manner. If you got any of this wrong, it could have tragic results. We are entrusted with the lives of the rest of the crew and passengers onboard. The job at most times entails consecutive long days working between sixteen and twenty-four hours straight traveling to and working in austere locations and environments. Most of the aircraft I flew on were about a decade older than me and were very uncomfortable. The cargo compartments could be very hot, extremely cold, and always smelled of jet fuel, hydraulic fluid, and engine exhaust, and that's just the good odors. The latrine facilities onboard were rough and would often fill up during the flight so it could be gross at times. My favorite aircraft I flew was the C-141 Starlifter. Its nickname was "the tube of pain" as it was loud, uncomfortable, and dark; however, I thought it was a terrific aircraft as it was dependable, powerful, and got me home safe throughout fifteen years and thousands of hours of flying it.

A big part of the challenge of being a transport crew-member was the lifestyle. Our diet was atrocious at best. We would often fly at night and sometimes eat breakfast three times in a twenty-four-hour period. During the flight, we were provided box lunches which were aptly nicknamed box nasties by the crews who had to eat them. Sometimes they were good but, often the disgruntled airmen responsible for feeding us just didn't care and their work reflected it. Some of box nasty hall of fame lunches included getting two slices of bread with peanut butter in between the slices with a packet of jelly on the side, pasta salad and a sandwich being packaged in the same container which would create this interesting soggy glob and undercooked chicken which was nicknamed "yard bird." There was a rule that the pilot and co-pilot couldn't eat the same meal during the flight and that was for good reason as you didn't want both people who could fly the airplane sick at the same time. My favorite box lunch had two Snickers, two Butterfingers, two bags of Doritos, two granola bars, and they had the audacity of putting two diet sodas with it.

Alcohol was prevalent with the job. It was normal for crew-members to have a drink or two or five after each flight while you were in crew rest and for some of the locations, there wasn't much to do other than drink. Even when we landed at home station, the crew would normally grab a beer or two and spend time debriefing maintenance personnel on the state of the aircraft and going over as a crew what went right and wrong during the mission and what we could do differently going forward. All our squadrons had beer refrigerators or vending machines stocked with beer, so alcohol was all around us and part of the lifestyle. I started flying at the age of eighteen, so I couldn't drink with my fellow crewmembers in the United States. But I would be able to partake during trips to most foreign countries where the drinking age was eighteen. By the time I'd turned twenty-one, I was pretty much done drinking and would almost always be the sober wingman and would volunteer to be the designated driver when we were lucky enough to have a vehicle.

The lifestyle could be perilous. In addition to the hazards of flying, the diet, and the alcohol, having a normal and consistent circadian rhythm was next to impossible as a crewmember. You were always operating in different time zones, sleeping on different schedules, and staying awake for very long stretches. We didn't even operate on local times, using Zulu time instead. Zulu time is used in the military and navigation for timekeeping purposes to avert confusion when coordinating with countries using other time standards. Time zones are measured as the number of hours offset from Greenwich Mean Time (GMT). For example, if it was 10:00 AM at Charleston Air Force Base in South Carolina, in Zulu time it would be 1400 Z or 2:00 PMZ. It is the same Zulu time everywhere in the world.

At times we had the ability to sleep on the aircraft during flight but on the C-141 it could be tough to sleep as it was loud and always very dry and hot in the bunks and they smelled of old cloth, sweat, and mildew. Our lodging was also inconsistent and while we did normally stay in decent hotels, changing hotels six times on a six-day trip can be challenging. On more than one occasion, I woke up in a very dark hotel room in a complete panic attack as I didn't know where I was, what country I was in, what the day was, what the time was, and didn't know the layout of the room and couldn't find a light switch. I ended up coming down with chronic insomnia near the end of my career, and I still battle with it today.

Boredom was a big factor in the job as there wasn't much to do at cruise altitude on long flights as this was a time before cell phones, tablets, computers, and handheld video game systems. Reading was really the only option to stay entertained, but you couldn't bring very many books or magazines with you as you were limited to what you could physically carry, and you had limited space for personal items in your flight suitcase and you also had a book bag with thirty pounds of military publications and a helmet bag with gear to carry. We rarely kept the same aircraft when flying on missions overseas so we couldn't store anything on the aircraft and had to take everything with us to the hotel. One of the constant sources of entertainment became practical jokes and while I probably could write an entire book just on that subject, I'll limit it to a couple of stories to make you laugh or cringe.

On the C-141 Starlifter we had a small panel on the floor of the flight deck that the Flight Engineer could open and view the avionics bay, which is an area with a bunch of computers that power and feed data to the hundreds of gauges and instruments on the aircraft. The bay is accessed through the toilet in the cargo compartment by removing a panel and there is enough room to enter and crouch down inside. During long flights we sometimes would invite passengers to visit the flight deck for a tour during the flight where they would normally spend about ten minutes speaking to the crew and learning about the aircraft, our routing, and all the gauges and controls.

This practical joke was called prisoners onboard. The Loadmaster on cue from the Flight Engineer would pre-position in the avionics bay with a chicken leg bone. Once the selected passenger settled in and sat down the Flight Engineer would open the avionics bay panel and throw down a whole chicken leg and within seconds the Loadmaster would toss up a chicken bone. This shocked everyone who fell prey to this joke, and they would start asking questions to figure out what was going on. The Flight Engineer would tell them the bottom of the aircraft was used as a prison cell when the military needed to transport prisoners between Europe and the United States. The gullible ones would ask to look in the bay and when this happened the Loadmaster would grab their foot and scare most victims senseless. I heard this practical joke was eventually retired on orders from senior leadership after a Loadmaster had his arm broken by a very frightened female officer. We would constantly do small jokes like adding dry ice to coffee, wearing silly nametags, telling passengers to look at the cargo to see if they could find some prop wash or flight line, but my favorite practical joke was 100 percent my creation, and I only did it once as I was concerned about getting court-martialed, which means brought up on legal charges.

In Charleston, we would fly airdrop missions in the late nights and early mornings and the Citadel, which is a local military college, would put their students on these flights as incentive rides. The students were usually very polite, motivated, professional, excited, and inquisitive. On one flight, this student who was probably my age got onboard and was very obnoxious and rude to me and was not very interested in the adventure and appeared to be very bored. He fell asleep in one of the troop seats in the cargo compartment before we even taxied to the runway. He slept through the low-level portion of the flight and remained asleep during the airdrop of the first pallet. I thought about shaking him awake but decided to play a practical joke instead and came up with this gem. I looped a cargo tiedown strap around his ankle and then tied a piece of string around the hook and tied the other end of the string to the next pallet which would be airdropped. A pallet which is airdropped is pulled out of the aircraft with a drag chute, and it leaves the cargo compartment at the speed you are flying which is normally over 120 miles per hour. As we started counting down for the green light, I woke him up at the three second mark and pointed at his leg in a very demonstrative manner. When the pallet departed the aircraft, it pulled the strap tight and gave his leg a nice little tug until the string broke and the strap slackened around his ankle. He stayed awake for the remainder of the flight and while that wasn't my finest judgement, it was very funny at the time.

Flying was also a lonely job and hard on the family as you are on the road between 100-250 days a year and calling home long distance from the road was very expensive and rarely done. Sometimes you would be scheduled for a short two- or three-day mission and would come home two weeks later and your family was very rarely notified correctly of the schedule change. Divorce percentages are high for transport crewmembers, and I was blessed to have a wife who was able to wear many hats and manage the rigors of my military aviation career.

The rigors of my career included staying current with all the latest information and getting tested and evaluated constantly, which was very stressful for me as even at this time I wasn't confident in my academic prowess. When you get good at being a basic qualified Loadmaster, they throw additional responsibilities at you including aeromedical, nuclear, special operations, and airdrop qualifications. Even with all that stress and the abnormal lifestyle, it turned out to be an amazing career choice, which I would not change for the world.

4
JOURNEY TO ADVENTURE

Flying is hours and hours of boredom sprinkled with a few seconds of sheer terror. —Pappy Boyington, U.S. Navy Aviator

After less than a year, I was sent back to Altus Air Force Base to complete airdrop training. This was a real shot in the gut as I was considered an average Loadmaster out of the several dozen airmen who were in the squadron and didn't have any sort of favorite status with leadership. They selected me to attend airdrop training a year or two earlier than all the others, and I would be the youngest and least experienced to attend from all four squadrons on the base. Being airdrop qualified meant that I would be home more often but it also meant fewer days off as most airdrop missions were training missions and were a day in duration so the schedulers could plug you into more missions. It also meant I would make less per diem each month, which is money they gave us for food when we traveled. Per diem was very important as the pay was so low and Suzan used this money to help pay bills. Most of all it was more learning, more studying, and more stress but with all that I was excited to attend and anxious to see how I would do during the classwork and flight training.

Basic airdrop qualification at the time consisted of first getting trained on how to airdrop paratroopers, which doesn't sound like it would be that difficult but there is more to it than just watching the paratroopers jump out of the aircraft. The biggest initial early hurdle is getting comfortable in opening the troop doors while flying 200 miles per hour at 800 feet off the ground. On the C-141, the Loadmaster would manually unlock and raise the troop door, electrically extend air deflectors which would cut down on the windblast for the paratroopers when they jumped and then extend by hand a small jump platform which the paratroopers would jump from when they exited the door. Once these items were moved in place, the Loadmaster would step outside of the airplane and stand on the platform to ensure everything was in good working order prior to handing the door over to the jumpmaster. On the ground, these tasks are all done very easily without much thought and effort, however, doing these tasks while the aircraft is bouncing all over the place during the low-level approach to the drop zone while wearing a helmet and parachute, dealing with the extra noise of open doors, dealing with extreme heat or cold add to the complexity and stress. Take all that and add the fact that there are two open doors in the back and, if you were to accidently fall out, it would likely mean death as the parachutes we used weren't very effective for low altitudes and we also received very minimal parachute training, which really ups the pucker factor. I totally respected those open doors, and it would probably have been easier to get a heard of cats into a bathtub at one time then it would have been for me to fall out of the plane. The best part was the super adrenaline rush and that part of the job never got old.

Flying on a NC-141A Starlifter over the Mojave Desert with the cargo doors open during a Test Pilot School mission in 1995

What did get old quick was low-level flying and doing it with paratroopers on board. Sometimes we would cram 160 paratroopers on the aircraft in four rows which meant these poor troops would have to sit sideways facing each other in red canvas troop seats with their legs intertwined. The space was so tight in this configuration, that the Loadmaster and Flight Engineer would often have to step on the troops while transitioning from the front of the aircraft to the back. The air-conditioning system would also be cut off to depressurize the aircraft prior to the low-level so when it was hot and humid outside, it was just as bad or worse inside. You also had those less than average box lunches or meals ready to eat, toilets that smelled, the heat causing you to sweat profusely from your head because everyone had to wear helmets. When you add all those factors along with the turbulence from the low-level flight, this made people get air sick and as the saying goes, when one paratrooper gets sick, they all get sick.

During my time flying airdrops, I would occasionally get sick and my diet during airdrop days mostly consisted of saltine crackers and cold water. One day I forgot I was flying an airdrop mission that evening and drank a bunch of milk and ate a very large meal, which is the worst thing you could do if you were prone to air sickness. It was a training mission which consisted of low-level flight segments followed by me throwing sandbags with small parachutes out of the troop doors. That night it was a total of three hours of flying with four sandbag drops at fifteen-minute intervals. It was a typical hot and humid summer night in Charleston and the ride was extra bumpy as there was turbulence during the low level. I was air sick by the time I got to the troop door and opened it for the first bundle drop. I took out an air sickness bag, filled it, took off my left glove and filled it, took off my right gloved and filled it and then moved my helmet to the side of my face, laid down on the cargo compartment floor with half of my body on the jump platform and my head sticking out into wind stream and threw up for the next fifteen minutes. I had the dry heaves during the remaining bundle drops but was able to accomplish the mission. After the drops, I was so weak, I could not stand up and had to crawl to the front of the airplane. To make matters worse, I had several Citadel cadets on board who were awake and witnessed the entire event. I'll chalk that up to karma for the practical joke I played on that Citadel cadet on an earlier airdrop mission. I was so sick that Suzan had to pick me up from the squadron. When we got home I didn't have the strength to walk up the stairs and crashed on our living room couch for two days.

Several years later I was flying on a flight test mission where I had to open the large cargo doors in the back and the test pilots were fighter pilots who were not used to flying cargo aircraft, so the flight was very rough. I had consumed a Hawaiian Punch soda right before the flight and when I started throwing up, the Flight Engineer told the pilot to declare an inflight emergency and land the plane. He thought I was throwing up blood. When I told them that I was okay and able to continue the flight, they decided to land as the pilots were getting sick as well, which is never good.

The Loadmaster's most important role in paratroop operations is during emergencies. While it's rare, occasionally, a paratrooper's parachute fails to deploy after they jump. This can be cause by improper rigging or even more rare and much worse is when their static line gets stuck between the aircraft and the jump platform. Either of these cases is bad and as the paratrooper stuck slightly below the aircraft which is flying 150 miles per hour and is continually slammed into the side and bottom of the aircraft. The Loadmaster's role is to identify and access the malfunction. For the hung static line, there is a small winch that is activated to pull in the jumper which must be done very carefully and with solid attention to detail. I was very blessed to have flown personnel air drop missions for two years and dropped thousands of paratroopers without ever experiencing any sort of malfunction. One of my friends was not so lucky and was on a mission where a static line wrapped around the neck of a paratrooper who was decapitated when the chute deployed. Over fifteen years of flying, we would occasionally have a cargo aircraft crash or someone would get seriously injured or die, which was tough, but you learned how to compartmentalize the bad news and press on with the mission.

The next phase of training was heavy equipment airdrop which was complex training as you had to learn all aspects of rigging, so you knew how to inspect the system to ensure everything was in working order and rigged correctly prior to takeoff. The rigging consisted of the main parachutes, static lines, harnesses, timers, and drag chute. You had to ensure everything was secured using the correct material ranging from string that would break with just five pounds of force to nylon cord which requires 550 pounds of force to break. If anything is rigged incorrectly, you risk a malfunction and a malfunction when dropping heavy equipment that weighted up to twenty tons from the back of a low altitude, low speed flying aircraft can and has been deadly.

Flying heavy equipment airdrops wasn't my favorite thing to do as most of the missions were training missions and up to three times a week you would go to work around 6:00 PM, have two hours of intense and sweaty work, fly a sixty-minute low level, drop a training pallet followed by another sixty-minute low level and another training pallet drop. We would then return to Charleston and do the same thing over again but this time dropping two sandbags instead of pallets. You would get home at about four in the morning and do it again the next day. Opening the large cargo doors in flight is a very neat experience and watching the cargo fly out of the plane at 150 miles per hour is also a huge rush especially when you had multiple pallets being dropped at the same time.

I had two dangerous incidents happen near the end of my time at Charleston while flying heavy equipment airdrop missions. The first was on an airdrop at Pope Air Force Base, North Carolina. We were dropping training pallets during the day, which was a nice change from all the night missions. We were getting ready to open the rear cargo doors and we had a hydraulic failure which is normally not that big of a deal because the C-141 has three hydraulic systems and each had a back-up. The real danger was we had leaking hydraulic fluid all over the floor and the fluid began to mist in the air. This is a not only a biohazard, but it can also be very flammable and could cause a fire or explosion. We donned our oxygen masks, turned the plane to land at the nearest airfield, which was Seymour Johnson Air Force Base, North Carolina, and began running emergency checklists.

We didn't have hydraulic power for the landing gear, so they had to be lowered using the manual procedure. This procedure was to remove small windows which were located by each of the landing gear in the back and the nose landing gear at the front of the aircraft. The Flight Engineer would then take a six-foot pry bar that we kept on the plane and pry each gear off the indention lock which would make gear freefall into place. The Flight Engineer was able to do this without any problems on the nose landing gear and the left main gear, but when he got to the right main landing gear, the cargo was in the way, and he did not have enough room to get the pry bar in place. The pry bar had a pin in the middle and the two halves of the bar could be disconnected as required. The remaining piece was about three feet long and weighted about thirty pounds and looked like a medieval spear. Immediately after sticking the pry bar out the landing gear access window, the Flight Engineer lost his grip and dropped it out of the aircraft. Lucky for us that we were over farmland as this thing was a metal spear falling at 150 miles per hour from 5,000 feet.

But the real issue now was that we no longer had the right tool to lower the right main landing gear, and we were getting low on fuel. The Flight Engineer spent the next thirty minutes using different poles we had on the aircraft until he was successful. Both of us moved to the flight deck where we unplugged from our portable oxygen bottles and plugged into the aircraft oxygen system. We landed safely at Seymour Johnson and, since we still had the fire and explosion risk, we evacuated the aircraft when we stopped up at the end of the runway to get out of danger and to hand the aircraft over to the fire department so they could do their thing. The hilarious thing is when I ran off the aircraft, I ended up stopping by a bunch of crew chiefs who were doing final pre-takeoff checks on a flight of F-4 aircraft which were getting ready to take off but couldn't since we had blocked the runway. Standing near me was David, my best friend from high school who I'd joined the Kentucky Air National Guard with. Yep, another Forrest Gump moment. He didn't recognize me as I had my helmet and oxygen mask on. We ended up connecting and had a nice evening and staying up all night reminiscing.

One of my final missions at Charleston and my very last airdrop mission in my career was a heavy equipment airdrop training mission once again at Pope Air Force Base. Instead of dropping training pallets, which were wood and cardboard, we were dropping two brand-new High Mobility Multipurpose Wheeled Vehicles (HMMWVs) which would go on to be called Humvees. These vehicles had just been introduced into service and were prized possessions. I was flying with a highly experienced Loadmaster who worked in the airdrop shop for several years and would go on to make Chief Master Sergeant. The vehicles would be dropped sequential, which means a drag chute would drop from the ceiling at the back of the aircraft and would pull the first vehicle out of the airplane. The second Humvee was connected to the first vehicle by a very long static line, and it would be pulled out by the first vehicle. The 12,000-pound combined load normally departs the aircraft in a matter of several seconds; however this mission would be far from normal.

We had completed the one-hour low level and the other Loadmaster had just opened the large cargo doors in the back of the aircraft. We were about seven minutes and twenty miles from the drop zone and had just started the final checklist prior to the airdrop, preparing our load for release over our drop zone. This consisted of ratcheting a handle at the front of the aircraft, which would detract the left side locks from the pallet. Once this happens, the pallets are being held in place just by the right locks, which have been adjusted to detract once the force of the drag chute pulls the first pallet out, then the second pallet is pulled out by the first.

As soon as the other Loadmaster retracted the left side locks, the pallet in the front, which was supposed to be the second pallet to exit the aircraft, started rolling to the rear. The other Loadmaster immediately notified the rest of the aircrew that we had a malfunction via the intercom system by stating "Malfunction, loose pallet." This pallet would roll into the pallet in the back and they both started rolling towards the back of the aircraft. If the pallets left the aircraft before schedule, it would have been very bad on multiple levels. First, we were still twenty miles from the drop zone and flying over civilian land. Second, the main cargo chutes would not deploy if the pallets rolled out of the aircraft prematurely. Both vehicles would exit the aircraft at more than 150 mph and fall 1,200 feet hitting the ground at several hundred miles per hour. Third, and most concerning, was the rear pallet was still connected to the aircraft via the drag chute which would be ripped from the ceiling of the aircraft by shear force and there are a lot of important things back there including the door controls, hydraulic lines, rudder, and flight controls.

After the second pallet started rolling, we both thought they would exit the aircraft, but they rolled to the very back of the aircraft and then abruptly stopped. The other Loadmaster notified the crew via the intercom system "first pallet is rolling, second pallet is rolling, they both are gone, oh crap they stopped." We both then immediately sprang into action and followed the malfunction checklist. There were tie-down chains pre-positioned on both sides of the aircraft for both pallets, which were there to secure the pallets in case of a malfunction. The issue was both vehicles rolled about thirty feet, so the chains were no longer in the correct spot. We both had to pick up the chains, move them thirty feet and secure both pallets. To make it more challenging, we were still flying the low level as we had to get to the drop zone in case the pallets exited the aircraft. It was a bumpy ride.

Once we had secured the pallets, the two of us quickly huddled and came up with a game plan. Our first action was to disconnect the drag chute as if it deployed, we would be in huge trouble as it would rip the pallets that were now chained to the aircraft out of the aircraft, and we would probably all die, and this is no exaggeration. We walked to the back of the aircraft and the other Loadmaster did something totally heroic. As I grabbed his legs, he stood on side wall of the aircraft, leaned over the pallet in the rear and disconnected the drag chute from the ceiling of the aircraft. The danger is amplified because we were on the ramp at the very rear of the aircraft with open cargo doors next to and behind us. We had the full force of the wind and noise which added to all the other stressors going on around us.

We were still very far from safe though, as we had two pallets at the tail end of the aircraft which created two dangerous situations. The first is we could not close the cargo doors and the second is we were flying way out of balance. An aircraft must fly with the balance point, its center of gravity, within several feet of the middle of the aircraft where the wings provide lift and we currently had six tons of cargo sitting as far from the middle as you could get. We had to come up with a plan of action and we didn't have a whole lot of time as we were limited on fuel. Our first plan was to remove the chains from the aft pallet and push it off the aircraft. An aircraft pallet is about seven feet long and about half of it was sticking off the aircraft ramp already. We tried with all our effort to push it out of the aircraft once were over the drop zone, but it would not budge. Our next plan was to connect the pallets together with chains and to use the cargo winch at the front of the aircraft to winch both pallets to the middle of the cargo floor to get the aircraft back into balance and to then shut the cargo doors.

We were able to move the pallets forward about ten feet when the winch stopped working. The other Loadmaster went forward to troubleshoot the winch while I started chaining the pallets back to the floor. The winch stopped working as the pallets were jammed as they had rolled over the bag which held over 100 feet of extraction line. About this time, the second Flight Engineer came downstairs and said that we were low on fuel and needed to return to Pope Air Force Base. The other Loadmaster told me to tie down the vehicles for landing, which would require a significant number of chains and devices and he would start working on the weight and balance. On the C-141, the Loadmaster calculates the center of gravity, which is used to adjust flight controls. Our normal maximum percentage is 33.4 percent of the mean aerodynamic chord and we would be landing at 44 percent. This is very technical, so the best way to explain it is we were going to land at a balance point that was way out of limits and something the aircraft wasn't designed for and something I'm not sure had ever been done before or since and this instability could easily cause uncontrollable flight during our landing attempt, which could result in a crash.

Within minutes of installing the final chain, we started our approach for landing. The pilot was incredible as we were landing with our cargo ramp down in the horizontal position and had to do a zero-flap landing, which means landing at a higher speed than usual. The pilot chose to use no flaps so our angle of attack would be flat, and we would not flare the nose up on touchdown as we would probably strike the tail of our aircraft onto the runway before the main landing gear came into contact. This could have damaged the aircraft or put us out of control. I wasn't scared at the time, but looking back at it decades later gives me the serious chills.

The pilot did an amazing job landing the aircraft and we did not scrape the tail. When he got to the end of the runway, he tried to turn onto the taxiway however our aircraft was so tail-heavy that our nose gear didn't have enough weight on it to turn the aircraft. The other Loadmaster directed me to open the crew entry door at the front of the aircraft and put the cargo struts down to prevent the aircraft from sitting on its tail which would likely damage the airplane.

I opened the door and extended the four-foot retractable ladder and it just swung as we were so tail-heavy it didn't reach the ground. I changed the plan and decided to exit out of a troop door in the back. I opened the door and jumped and was shocked at the short travel distance to the ground. The jump was normally about five feet but could be more or depending on how much fuel and cargo were on the aircraft. I hit the ground after about a three-foot drop. The struts on the C-141 can be accessed through small panels on each side near the cargo ramp and are pulled out and swung into place. You normally press on a tab and lower them into place before locking them into position with a valve. As I swung the first strut, I quickly came to the realization that we were too low in the back of the aircraft to deploy these which made me even more impressed with the job the pilot did both flying and landing the aircraft safely.

The drama was over rather rapidly after that. Our pallets were offloaded, we were towed off the runway, fueled, and took off for the short flight back to Charleston. We'd all thought we were going to return as heroes; however, we were sadly mistaken and were subjected to poor culture, poor leadership, and bureaucracy. Immediately after landing we were met by multiple teams including safety, standardization and evaluation, maintenance, and aerial delivery. The aerial delivery team quickly found out what the problem was. The locks on the right-hand side of the cargo floor malfunctioned and instead of being good for 4,000 pounds of restraint, they were essentially useless as you could take your foot and jiggle each lock and the locking mechanism would fail. Apparently, this had been found on several other aircraft in the days prior to this incident. The disappointing thing is instead of receiving an attaboy or even encouragement we were victims of "guilty until proven innocent" mentality. We were told that we should consider ourselves Q3 which meant unqualified. All our scheduled missions were cancelled, and we were told to wait by the phone at home until we heard something.

What I learned from this event is leadership matters and people are our greatest asset. The leadership, bravery, and calmness shown by the other Loadmaster still inspires me today and the leadership and technical ability displayed by that Air Force Reserve pilot was incredible. The entire crew came together and performed admirably and saved that aircraft and each other. I would go on to leave Charleston just months later and requested this same crew to be on my final flight. Just as I learned so much about teamwork, commitment, and professionalism from this crew, I also learned what not to do from the bureaucrats who were too consumed with their processes and too into intimidating people that they forgot or didn't care about the people element. We would go on to receive a thank you letter from the 82nd Airborne Division Commanding General for saving their new Hummers, and we were submitted for Air Medals. While it didn't really matter to me at the time, the Air Medals were downgraded to Air Force Commendation Medals. Looking back, I really think the other Loadmaster and Pilot were deserving of the Air Medal or higher. I believe we were probably a victim of timing as Desert Shield has just started and I don't believe the bureaucrats wanted to give an Air Medal in wartime for something that happened in training. My Commendation Medal was pinned on me over a year later by my Group Commander, Colonel James Doolittle, who was grandson of General Jimmy Doolittle. He mentioned on stage that it was an absolute shame that he was not pinning a Distinguished Flying Cross on me because the entire crew deserved it.

Charleston had been a solid first assignment. I had qualified on the aircraft in good time, picked up the airdrop qualification in record time, and participated in multiple important missions including flying supplies to the Soviet Union near the end of the cold war to support the Intermediate-Range Nuclear Forces Treaty teams and flew multiple missions to support in the invasion of Panama during Operation Just Cause. I was eighteen when I arrived and twenty-one when I departed and I'd learned so much about the Air Force, leadership, followership, aviation, people, geography, and history during these years. This was a much better education then I would have ever received in college.

Most strategic aircraft Loadmasters during my era spent their entire career flying at one base. A few would be selected for instructor duty at Altus and would often return to the location of their initial duty assignment after three years. My path was going to be very different. I had the opportunity to meet one of my first mentors and champions. Chief Master Sergeant Bob Gilbert was our most senior Flight Engineer in my squadron at Charleston Air Force Base and he had become a legend for helping develop a piece of ground equipment which could extract fuel out of an aircraft to fuel another aircraft. It would later be used at Desert One during Operation Eagle Claw, the failed operation to free the fifty-two American Embassy Hostages in Iran in 1980. Chief Gilbert was not your traditional Air Force Chief. He was not politically correct, participated in motocross, and really didn't like following the status quo.

Chief Gilbert had been selected to become the senior enlisted aviator for 4950th Test Wing at Wright-Patterson Air Force Base in Ohio. The Chief had taken me under his wing because he liked my determination, work ethic, and ability to bend the rules when it made sense. When the Chief arrived at Wright-Patterson, he quickly noticed that most of the aviators in the squadron were significantly older, had been in flight test for many years, had lost some of their zeal, and were largely biding their time to retire. In the military we call this Retried On Active Duty or R O A D. The Chief handpicked me, and a young Staff Sergeant Flight Engineer named Russ Brown to fill two open billets. This was a very big deal for me as I was a brand-new E-4 and would be filling an E-7 billet. I don't believe the folks at the Air Force Personnel Center were very happy with this idea and the other enlisted aviators in my new unit were even less happy as when I applied for the position—they threw my resume in the trash. The Chief wasn't having any of it and made it happen so, after three years at Charleston, me, Suzan and our new baby James packed up and moved to Ohio. What I learned from Chief Gilbert is kindness matters and success allows you to challenge the status quo.

When I arrived at Wright-Patterson Air Force Base, it was more than clear that this was going to be a much different assignment. At Charleston we'd had 45+ C-141B Starlifters with close to 300 Loadmasters, and at Wright-Patterson we had four older and unstretched C-141A Starlifters and just three Loadmasters. I was going to have to prove myself as I was the youngest enlisted aviator by a good ten years, and my flying mates had nicknamed me Junior. This assignment was supposed to provide more stability as I was assigned an office job and would fly just once or twice a week and would rarely have to be away from home, however this was right at the beginning of Desert Shield and things were getting ready to get crazy busy.

In 1991 our flight test squadron was selected to fly missions to locations normally supported by Air Mobility Command whose aircraft were now extremely busy flying missions from the United States and Europe to the Middle East to support the 697,000 American Troops who were deployed for Desert Shield soon to followed by Desert Storm. We were selected to fill the gap and fly supply missions to military bases in Greenland, Iceland, Puerto Rico, Panama, Bermuda, and the Azores and to support Department of State Embassies at other locations including Kenya, Brazil, and Argentina. We also flew strategic missions to large military bases in Germany, England, and Italy to support the war and flew one mission into the combat theater delivering a field hospital to Saudi Arabia.

We only had three Loadmasters and we committed to fly two aircraft for Air Mobility Command missions, so I was extremely busy. I was lucky because I didn't deploy for six months or a year at a time like many, but I was gone a lot for most of 1991. I would leave for a week or two and come home for a week and leave again for a week or two. There were multiple times where I was gone for two weeks, came home for a day and left for another two weeks. I was able to see James take his first steps during one these short layovers at home. I know that I was blessed that I wasn't gone for a long continuous period, but it did take a toll on my young family. It also took a toll on the crews as well. We were flying two of the oldest Starlifters built and they had not been modified with any of the new technology including communication and navigation and did not have any crew bunks installed in the cargo compartment. For navigation, we often used a sextant and navigated like sailors did 300 years ago. Crew bunks don't sound to important, but when you are flying sixteen- to twenty-four-hour days back-to-back with only twelve hours of crew rest in between, getting several hours of sleep during flight is very important. We did adapt and sucked it up for the year and I'm very proud of the contributions my squadron made during the war.

I had an amazing Squadron Commander at Wright-Patterson from whom I learned valuable lessons that would serve me well in years to come. General Raymond Johns was a flight test pilot, and during my time at Wright-Patterson he was the test pilot for the brand-new VC-25As which are the two Boeing 747s still used today for Air Force One missions. Colonel Johns at the time was what I call a right-hand turn aircraft commander. When pilots get on board a cargo aircraft, they climb the first crew ladder and most immediately take a left-hand turn to go up the second ladder and climb up to the flight deck. The good ones will take a right-hand turn and go talk to the Loadmaster to find out how things were progressing with aircraft servicing, cargo operations, passenger operations, customs, and immigration. Colonel Johns would always make that right-hand turn and come talk to me. He understood that the aircraft's mission had to do with everything to the right of the main door and not the left. At the office, senior leadership sat upstairs, and the junior pilots and enlisted crew sat in the basement. Colonel Johns would come downstairs once a week to check on everyone and he knew the names of kids and spouses. He even visited me during an overnight stay at the hospital when I had my wisdom teeth removed and came to a welcome party which was thrown at my house unannounced.

I did have a unique run in with the Colonel while flying missions during Desert Storm.

During a mission with a stop in Lajes Air Base, Azores, we were delayed by the notorious heavy crosswinds on the island. After waiting for many hours and the decision to fly was changed several times, the enlisted crew spoke up and made the call to inform the Colonel as aircraft commander that we thought prudent safety protocols called for us to delay the mission by fifteen hours and enter crew rest and wait for the weather to improve before we attempted a takeoff. The Colonel was very displeased, but his hands were very much tied since we'd played the safety card. To his credit, later in the trip, he apologized to each one of us and backed our call as the right thing to do. What I learned from him is people are the most important asset and making time to take care of your people will pay dividends.

Over twenty-five years later, General Ray Johns as the Commander of Air Mobility Command would visit UPS Global Headquarters in Atlanta and I attended the meeting as UPS Director of Global Government Operations. I was the youngest and most junior UPSer in the room and seated at the far end of a very long table in the executive conference room. General Johns sat down at the table next to our CEO and looked at me and said "Junior, what are you doing way down there" and invited me to sit next to him. He had me explain how I got the name Junior and about our time flying together in Desert Storm. What a class act!

When I moved to Wright-Patterson, I was told we'd probably be there for my entire career, but due to the Base Realignment and Closures Commission, the entire flight test wing at Wright-Patterson was relocated to Edwards Air Force Base, California. Edwards is in the middle of the Mojave Desert and sits between Barstow and Bakersfield and is about 100 miles east of Los

Angeles. The base is known for Space Shuttle landings and has supported flight test operations since the late 1940s.

Edwards is in an extremely large and desolate area and the base is very remote. It takes about twenty minutes to drive off the base from any of the three gates and about forty-five minutes to get to the nearest Walmart. The remoteness, harsh landscape, and extremely high heat can be shocking to those who have never been in a desert. The going advice at the time was to drive your family into the base at night so they wouldn't be aware of just how bad it the conditions were. I didn't take that advice when we drove from Ohio, and it was quite shocking for Suzan. She spent the first two days in the corner of our hotel room crying. Before we left Ohio, they had a spouse day where they brought the families in and gave them an overview of the base and surrounding area. It ended up being total nonsense as they highlighted officer housing and kept showing grass and green trees throughout the slide show. Edwards doesn't have much grass or trees and I never knew that brown came in so many shades. We initially moved on to Boron, California, as the housing offered to us on base was beyond bad. The base up until the mid-'90s had almost been forgotten, the investment in infrastructure had been almost non-existent, and 95 percent of the enlisted base housing was just pathetic. Boron was rough as well and it was a thirty-minute drive to get on the base, and over and hour to get to a McDonalds and Walmart.

The area and assignment did grow on us as we found amazing friends and made terrific memories including the arrival of our youngest son Brandon several years after we arrived. The high desert is also a special area with amazing sunsets and cool temperatures in the evening, but the 115° summer days were brutal. It was about two hours from Los Angles and although we were poor, we were able to score discounted military tickets and spend good quality family time at Disneyland,

Knotts Berry Farm, and Universal Studio, and we took multiple vacations to Las Vegas.

As an aviation buff, spending five years at Edwards was amazing. In addition to being qualified on the C41A Starlifter, I went back to Altus to become qualified on the C-5 Galaxy and went to US Army Flight Engineer School and became qualified on the C-23 Sherpa Aircraft. The C-5 is like a flying warehouse with a maximum takeoff weight of 762,000 pounds and the C-23, which is a plane built in Ireland, looks like a Winnebago with wings. I was also able fly on several different planes including the T-37 Tweet, T-39 Saberliner, and C-135 Stratolifter.

I took part in some very cool and dangerous flight test missions including having an F-15 aircraft shoot missiles at our aircraft to test out different missile warning systems. I flew several missions that evaluated new automatic landing systems which are now on every modern plane but at the time the technology was new, and the missions were somewhat dangerous. We also had one of the C-141 Starlifters retrofitted with electric flight controls which was previously done on a C-130 aircraft that had crashed and killed everyone onboard. Every day at Edwards was like an airshow with cool test programs going on including the B-2 Stealth Bomber and F-22 Raptor. We saw the space shuttle land many times and NASA was even flying the SR-71 Blackbird. I flew missions to wonderful areas including Hawaii, Japan, South Korea, Saipan, Kwajalein Atoll, Wake Island, Brazil, Costa Rica, and Panama. I was also selected to take part in two air shows with Chuck Yeager.

Brigadier General Charles Elwood Yeager was an Air Force Ace and renowned test pilot who became the first person to break the sound barrier. He was a living legend in the flight test community and even though he was retired he was allowed to fly most of the aircraft assigned to Edwards AFB. The first time I met him I was in complete awe as he was one of my heroes growing up. I was very impressed and while he was a bit hard of hearing and very old school, he was an incredible pilot and very genuine. During my time at Edwards AFB, he would fly an F-15 each year at our annual air show and break the sound barrier.

During these airshows, I was flying the C-23 Sherpa that would drop the Air Force Academy Wings of Blue team for the flag ceremony and immediately afterwards General Yeager would break the sound barrier. In 1997, during the 50th Air Force Anniversary Air Show, we were having our pre-flight briefings at the Air Force Test Pilot School, which took about an hour and long and tedious. With about twenty minutes remaining, General Yeager had enough of the briefings and left the auditorium. When it came time to take the van out to our plane, we couldn't find him anywhere and eventually had to leave so we wouldn't be late and delay the show. As we were driving through the crowd, we spotted General Yeager who apparently had decided to walk to the aircraft and was mobbed by the crowd. He was in great shape as he had probably walked close to two miles by the time, we caught up to him. During my professional careers in the Air Force and in corporate world, I learned a lot by observing and what I learned from Chuck Yeager was confidence is okay if it's tapered with genuineness and backed with ability.

My next assignment was important in maturing and getting what we in the Air Force called re-blued which means being remotivated in Air Force culture and mission. I was selected for a four-year assignment to the 623rd Air Mobility Squadron in Ramstein Air Base, Germany, to join a TALCE unit. TALCE stands for Tanker Airlift Control Element and is a deployable unit with two missions. The first is to set up command and control operations at commercial airfields or foreign military bases and the second is to teach aircraft load planning to U.S. and

NATO units in Europe. Both are amazing missions and the experience I gained at the TALCE served me well for years to come.

In this job I figured out that the cargo in the back of my plane was very important as people relied on this cargo, which needed to be delivered undamaged and on-time. I figured out during this assignment that flying was just a cog in the logistics wheel and just one part of the Air Force mission. As I mentioned earlier, I'm a foodie and during a mission to a remote base in the Middle East, we had the opportunity to have a meal at an Air Force field kitchen that was set up near the flight line in a tent. It was once again time to eat breakfast and I ordered French toast, and the incredibly nice cook told me that we had just delivered bread and eggs and he needed to grab them off the pallet that was now sitting behind tent in order to make my breakfast.

The second thing I had to figure out was how to become a classroom teacher. I still didn't think I was very smart, but through hard work and the mentorship of several rock-solid noncommissioned officers, I did well and within three years became the chief instructor for the unit. With this mentorship, I'd discovered that I enjoyed teaching and was an was an effective instructor because I was able to make instruction fun, cared for my students, and had high expectations of myself, my fellow instructors, and my students.

During this assignment I learned positive attributes from several more seasoned TALCE non-commissioned officers but I also learned what not to be like from several others who were obnoxiously self-centered and had integrity issues. Several others in the unit had poor people skills and the unit while in garrison was dysfunctional at best. However, when we deployed, all that was out the window and I've never seen a group of harder working men and women in my life. We would get the mission done and the job, while incredibly exhausting, was also fun at times.

Two of the best noncommissioned officers during this assignment would go on to do very well in the Air Force but would unfortunately pass away shortly after retirement. I'll never forget Operations Specialist Todd Lewis and my good friend Boom Operator Jeff Sidles. I learned from Jeff the importance of a sense of humor and how staying calm as a leader was contagious. Jeff passed away just a couple of months after Suzan, and it was another big hurt as we had become good friends and were stationed together again several years after Germany and stayed in touch over the years even after we both retired. In Todd I saw this amazing passion and love for the Air Force that was unapparelled. I miss you both and may you rest in peace, and I pray that you have connected in heaven.

Suzan and my boys spent four years in Germany, and I probably only spent two as I was gone constantly. This job was far different from flying cargo planes as we would spend weeks and sometimes months at a single location. My Army veteran buddies always cringe when I use the term deployed as we usually deployed in style in the Air Force compared to our sister services. I was deployed and going on temporary duty assignments constantly supporting peacekeeping, humanitarian, and training missions in Kenya, Turkey, Jordan, Spain, Kenya, South Africa, and Bulgaria and teaching throughout Germany and Italy and attending training classes and flying back in the United States. I had to maintain my flight status in this job which meant flying every sixty days regardless of what was going on or how busy my schedule was.

On Sep 11, 2001 my entire squadron sat in the operations room and watched the tragic events of 9-11 unfold on Armed Forces Network for several hours before we all rushed home to pack and spend time with our families as we knew our lives would be different going forward. Because the TALCE was at the tip of the spear, we expected to be sent on lengthy deployments in the very near future. This was true for almost my entire unit except for me as I had a slot for the Non-Commissioned Officers Academy at Kapaun Air Station outside of Ramstein a month after 9-11. I pleaded to get out of the academy slot and deploy with my team, but my request was not approved.

While I had had some academic success attending flight schools, I didn't have a lot of confidence going into the academy as I had not completed any college, hadn't supervised many airmen, and really wasn't that gung-ho since I had been in aviation units for most of my career. I ended up loving the NCO Academy and gained a tremendous amount of knowledge which increased my abilities and confidence. I learned about a multitude of topics including leadership, followership, communication, speech writing, critical writing, public speaking, and conflict management, which would serve me well for this and future endeavors. I found out that I was a decent writer and pretty good at giving speeches and in Air Force Professional Military Education (PME) there are a lot of paper writing and speech assignments. I often joke about this today. In Marine Corps professional military education, they teach Marines how to kill the enemy better, Navy teaches sailors how to better navigate at sea and put out fires, Army teaches soldiers how to be better at land navigation, and Air Force teaches airmen how to give speeches and write papers and properly hold a teacup and which fork to use during dinner.

I went into the NCO Academy with a positive attitude and gave it my all by studying like mad, volunteering for additional opportunities, leading teams, and mentoring fellow NCOs who were struggling with their papers and speeches. I also observed and learned from highly effective and more experienced NCOs and openly accepted mentorship from my instructors.

In one of the best memories I have, which was even better because Suzan was by my side, at the NCO Academy graduation I received the Distinguished Graduate Award and the Commandant's Award for Leadership. All things are possible with God, and he was guiding me on my journey to VETLANTA.

The four years in Germany was amazing and so special for Suzan. She was able to land her dream job as a veterinarian technician. She became a rock star because of her personality and performance at the vet clinic. She was stopped wherever we wont to talk about people's pets and give advice. She worked for a boss she really liked, and she threw herself into this new career and completed US Army Veterinarian Certification by correspondence. We made amazing friends and took outstanding vacations to areas she fantasied about including Germany, Czech Republic, Holland, England, Italy, Austria, Poland, Switzerland, Belgium, and France. We even spent our last night in Germany in a castle hotel on the Rhine River.

We rotated back to the U.S. after lobbying hard for a Headquarters Air Mobility Command assignment and were sent to Scott Air Force Base, Illinois, which is approximately fifteen miles east of St. Louis. This was my first assignment where I didn't have to maintain flight status and while I didn't know it at the time, my flying career was over with my last flight as a Loadmaster in 2002. I had been on flight status for fifteen years, logging over 2,000 flight hours, and traveled to over sixty countries. I took part in every major military operation including Operation Just Cause in Panama, Operations Desert Shield, Desert Storm, and Southern Watch and Northern Watch in Iraq. On the plane, I carried a diverse amount of cargo over the years including dolphins, cats, dogs, California Condors, dynamite, bombs, patients, supplies, food, weapons, dignitaries, family members, veterans, warriors, and everything in between. I saw so much of the world with highlights including seeing the

Moai Heads in Easter Island, snorkeling in Hanauma Bay Hawaii, crossing Checkpoint Charlie in Berlin, seeing the Northern Lights dozens of times in Alaska, Greenland, and Iceland, seeing St. Elmo's Fire on the windshield of the aircraft, seeing moose walk up to the aircraft in Alaska, walking inside the pyramids and seeing the King Tut exhibit in a museum in Egypt, taking safaris in Kenya and South Africa, visiting palaces and castles in England, Germany, and France and walking on WWII sites in Germany, France, Holland, Belgium, Luxemburg, Italy, Saipan, and Wake Island. I flew over amazing sites including seeing lava flowing from Mount Etna in Italy, the Panama and Suez Canals, the Statue of Liberty, Mount Rushmore, the Amazon and Nile Rivers, and the Eifel Tower. I'm so blessed to have seen the world and even more blessed that I always gotten to return home to the United States of America, the greatest country in the world and to my beautiful bride and kids.

This new job was much different than anything else I had done to this point. I completed an eighteen-month assignment at the Tanker Airlift Control Center (TACC) where I oversaw deployments of C-130 and C-21 aviation units to Central Command to support the second gulf war and eighteen months as the TALCE Training Functional Manager on the AMC staff where my biggest battle was the daily grind of navigating all the red tape and bureaucracy.

During my time at Scott AFB, I had the opportunity to raise my hand and become the Security Manager at TACC, which would help me land my next career at UPS five years later, become the Booster Club Presidents for TACC and HQ AMC, and become a fill-in First Sergeant, commonly referred to as "under shirt." I was blessed at this assignment as I made Mater Sergeant (E-7) on my very first attempt and was recognized as Non-Commissioned Officer of the Year at TACC and Senior Non-Commissioned Officer of the Year at HQ AMC. The interesting thing is these were the very first awards I had ever won outside of an academic situation in my entire career. I'm thankful to my leadership who recognized my efforts and spent the time writing effective award packages.

This was my first non-flying assignment, and outside of short trips, I was home for most of my three years. This was an adjustment for me and the family, but it ended up being fantastic. I wasn't tired all the time, and I was able to spend more time with the family and help Suzan around the house including cooking, which I absolutely love to do. I was also able to spend serous time on self-development and started taking college courses and finished two Community College of the Air Force Associate Degrees and a bachelor's degree from American Military University.

I also found solid mentors for the first time in my career including my brother John who was the noncommissioned officer in charge at the Scott Air Force Base Dental Clinic and then a First Sergeant at the Mission Support Squadron and then the Air Base Operations Group. My mentors including John were all First Sergeants who put me on a very different path than most enlisted aviators at the time.

5
JOURNEY TO LEADERSHIP

When you're First Sergeant, you're a role model whether you know it or not. You're a role model for the person that will be in your job. Not next month or next year, but ten years from now. Every day soldiers are watching you and deciding if you are the kind of First Sergeant they want to be. –An Army First Sergeant, 1988

I really liked being a fill in First Sergeant and soon completed the Air Force First Sergeants Academy by correspondence and was encouraged by my brother and other mentors to apply for a special duty assignment to become a full-time First Sergeant. Our base commander at the time had served on the E-9 promotion board and debriefed the senior non-commissioned officers on the base and provided advice on how to improve your board scores. At the top of the list was to complete special duty assignments such as First Sergeant, Recruiter, and Technical Instructor. That gave me the push to formally apply, which consisted of a medical records review, mental health evaluation, physical fitness test, and a recommendation for the First Sergeants Council which my brother chaired at the time.

I flew through the approval process and was promptly turned down by my career functional managers at the Air Force Personnel Center as they advised enlisted aviators could not be selected for special duty assignments outside of their career field. I promptly sent them a copy of the base commander's slides and mentioned that the first Chief Master Sergeant of the Air, Paul Airey, who was an aircraft gunner and the fourth, Thomas Barnes, who was a Flight Engineer would be very disappointed to hear there would never be another enlisted aviator eligible for this position due to this policy. I'm still surprised even today that they changed their minds and I won my final red tape battle at Headquarters Air Mobility Command.

First sergeants advise commanders on the readiness, health, morale, welfare, and quality of life of Airmen and families to ensure a mission-ready force (Air Force Fact Sheet). Suzan best described the First Sergeant as the mother of the squadron. The father (the commander) is often gone or occupied with other roles and responsibilities, so the First Sergeant is there to provide attention and discipline and to ensure everything is orderly and done properly.

The rank of First Sergeant has existed in the American Army since 1781, when a fifth sergeant was added to the table of organization for Continental Army infantry regiments. Previously, under the tables of organization approved by the Continental Congress in 1776 and 1779, there were four and three sergeants, respectively, authorized in each company. The sergeants were numbered in order of seniority, and the "first" sergeant was simply the senior sergeant in the company, but not a separate rank. After the 1781 Battle of Green Spring, Ebenezer Denny called the company first sergeant "the most important officer." In the Air Force First Sergeants are often called "shirt." There are several theories on why, but my favorite is during military service in frontier times, federal troops often had tattered uniforms as they were not routinely resupplied. When the supply wagon would arrive with new uniforms, the first sergeant, would get the first pick of shirts. The motto of the Air Force First Sergeant is "People Are Our Business" and the job is all about people: the good, the bad, and the ugly.

There were so many good elements of the job including troops getting promoted or selected for special assignments, getting the mission accomplished especially during deployments, attending college and professional military education graduations, helping troops and their families through issues and fighting for my troops when they deserved better. The bad included making death notifications when a family member had passed away, separating good airmen who could not pass their upgrade training after technical school, separating troops who made bad financial decisions and no longer qualified for a security clearance.

The ugly included reviewing every quarter all the suicides in the command, overseeing domestic violence cases including child abuse, dealing with legal issues including a rash of DUIs and motorcycle accidents. The ugly also consisted of dealing with the occasional troop that was just evil and I don't use this term lightly or indiscriminately. There are very bad people in this world, and some find their way into the military. They are often extremely entitled individuals whose only concerns are there wellbeing, pleasure, and the gratification they have when they make everyone around them miserable. We all have worked with folks like these, but in the military, they are much more disruptive and their impact on morale, welfare, and esprit de corps puts the mission and lives in jeopardy.

In the beginning of my time as a First Sergeant, I thought I could rescue these individuals or at least provide solid mentorship that would change their behaviors enough to mitigate their disruption. I believe I was really a good fit for the position and excelled at it. I loved mentoring troops and junior officers and tried to spend 90 percent of my time dealing with the top 90 percent of the force and not 90 percent of my time on the bottom 10 percent. Trying to rescue or mentor these evildoers means you end up spending 90 percent of your time with the very bottom tenth of a percent.

About a decade later while at UPS, I would receive the best advice on how to deal with these people from my former base commander at Scott Air Force Base, Darren McDew, who went on to get promoted to Four Star General and became the commander at Air Mobility Command and then U.S. Transportation Command. He visited UPS to take a tour of our operations and gave an incredible speech in front of our leadership, Veterans Business Resource Group, and African American Business Resource Group at the Muhammad Ali Center in Louisville, Kentucky. He called the evil, "deadwood" and advised that our job as leaders is to stop trying to save these people and to cut them loose from your organization. He has a version of this speech on YouTube if you want to check it out. https://www.youtube.com/watch?v=PQ-isj0GCiQ

The Air Force has a First Sergeants Academy, and they do a nice job of providing a foundation for the challenges of the position. The academy is at Gunter Annex, Maxwell AFB, Alabama, where the resident learning course consists of 190 hours and is divided into four weeks of demanding curriculum, including First Sergeant Responsibilities, Maintenance and Discipline, Negotiation and Dispute Resolution, Resiliency Training, and First Sergeant Legal Orientation ost of the job however is figured out while doing it as there is just a myriad of people issues which you face. At Scott AFB, the First Sergeant Council met every Friday after work at the base club for refreshments. It was called choir practice because we would sing to each other about the week we had and the challenges we faced.

The typical opening was "you are not going to believe what a troop in my squadron did this week." These meetings became very important in establishing relationships with the other First Sergeants, decompressing before you went home to the family for the weekend, and to learn new tips, techniques, and resources. I always wanted to write a book and title it *Stories from First Sergeants* so maybe that's next.

The job was challenging, exhausting, incredible, and all-encompassing at times. There were more emotions with this job than any other in my life including joy, anxiety, anger, fear, empathy, heartbreak, disgust, satisfaction, annoyance, self-confidence, pride, disappointment, amusement, gratitude, enthusiasm, pessimism, and grief. I have sad stories, funny stories, inspirational stories, and shocking stories, but I'll share something funny that happened early on in my First Sergeant Career. As I mentioned, my brother John was a First Sergeant, and we were assigned together at Scott Air Force Base.

Each year the First Sergeants around the Air Force meet at a conference and most of the shirts at Scott Air Force Base attended this particular year. Normally when the First Sergeant is out of the office, a senior noncommissioned officer in the squadron who is selected and trained to be the under First Sergeant will fill in. My brother did not have anyone in his squadron who had been suitably trained so he asked me to fill in for him and since it was just for a couple of days and they had no major issues going on, I accepted. On the very first night, he called from the road and said he had a spouse whose husband was deployed, and she had injured herself at home and while the injury was minor, she was at the hospital, and he asked me if I could visit. She apparently had a long history of seeking attention while her husband was deployed and made every effort to try get him returned home so this was likely something similar and he believed a visit from me would help calm her down.

I put on my uniform and went to the base hospital and had a very nice visit. Her injuries were minor, and I reinforced that her husband's deployment would end soon and reviewed all the resources available to support her and their family. I didn't mention that John was my brother, and we have different last names, so she didn't know. The last thing she said to me as I was leaving was that I was so much nicer than Senior Master Sergeant Solomon as he was mean and a big jerk. I defended my brother saying that we just had different styles and he cared for his troops and their families very much, meanwhile, I was cracking up inside. I wanted to tell her that she didn't have to tell me that he was mean as he used to beat me up when we were kids. My mom loves this story and we all still laugh at it twenty years later. During this assignment I learned from my brother the importance of surrounding yourself with capable people as there will be times you will need to lean on each other, and the best mentors can be with your peers. I also learned that leadership at times takes directness and candor, and he had an abundance of both.

When I graduated from the First Sergeants Academy and sewed on my diamond, I was given orders to the Fourth Communications Squadron at Seymour Johnson Air Force Base, North Carolina. Seymour Johnson is an F-15 Eagle base near Goldsboro and is often referred to as "Shady J." It's the only military installation named after a person from a different military branch. The base is named for US Navy Lt. Seymour A. Johnson, a test pilot from Goldsboro who died in an airplane crash in Maryland in 1941. Goldsboro is an interesting town that I honestly didn't think much of. Entering the town there was a sign that said "Goldsboro, Best small town to live in 1980." I always joked around and said they rested on their laurels after they won that award because the town had become stagnant for years.

The highlight of my time at "Shady J" was my commander, Lieutenant Colonel Stamatis Smeltz. He was half Greek and had been exposed to some wonderful Air Force mentors as a child in Greece. We had a fantastic relationship during our two years serving together and, without a doubt, he was my best commander. I'm going to butcher some of his lessons, but here goes. He would often close out commander calls with "you are all near and dear to someone, so please take care of yourself." He borrowed this from one of his college professors, but it worked well in the Air Force, and I've used this many times in my civilian career and volunteer roles. If you've ever worked for me or with me, you've probably heard me say this way too many times and it came right from Colonel Smeltz. Success is a matter of many factors including good luck, good timing, a good boss, and good performance and never forget that good performance is the only one of these factors in your direct control.

Fourth Communications Squadron Commander Lieutenant Colonel Stamatis Smeltz and First Sergeant Lloyd Knight in 2006

I tested for promotion to Senior Master Sergeant just once and it was as a First Sergeant which was highly competitive and frankly it stressed me out as I had studied for ten months and had put my all into it. I ended up missing it by less than two points and had the second highest board score and test points without getting promoted in the entire Air Force for that year. If you are not familiar with the way promotions work in the Air Force, here is a quick breakdown for this period. You would get two points for ever year of service, six points for every year in grade, up to 26 points for medals, up to 100 points for a test in your career field, and up to 100 points for a test in general Air Force knowledge and, for promotion to E-8 and E-9, your records would meet a board comprised of two Chief Master Sergeants and a full bird Colonel. They'd each review your records and individually calculate a score and the tabulated board score will be between 270 and 450 points.

I had an amazing board score driven by past performance, the diversity of roles and responsibilities I had taken, along with the awards, education, and self-development pursuits I had conducted. Attending the Senior Non-Commissioned Officer Academy was a goal of mine for many years, so I was thrilled to be attending even if I hadn't been promoted. The Air Force Senior Non-Commissioned Officer Academy is the third level of enlisted professional military education. The Senior NCO Academy is located Gunter Annex, which is a small installation operated by Maxwell Air Force Base, and both are in Montgomery, Alabama. The academy curriculum consists of 200 classroom hours, which prepares senior NCOs to lead the enlisted force in the employment of air and space power in support of US national security objectives. The program is delivered in 25 academic days and there are 6 classes each year with approximately 300 students in each class.

Most of the students are Air Force but there are also a handful of students and instructors from the other military branches and foreign military students. My class had two Japanese Air Self-Defense Senior Master Sergeants who were probably the oldest students in attendance but also the most physically fit. They smoked all of us during every run and anything we did fitness wise. They however did have a penchant in sleeping and snoring during seminars. In my group, we had an Army Command Sergeant Major who oversaw recruiting in the southeast.

The Air Force Senior NCO Academy was popular with Army Sergeant Majors as their Senior NCO Academy is nine months long. In my cohort at the academy, we had an Army Command Sergeant Major and 19 airmen. The Command Sergeant Major introduced himself in an over-the-top gung-ho manner and threatened the Air Force students not to call him by his first name, Sarge, or Sergeant. The fantastic thing is he was so impressed with the curriculum and the fellow students that we all bonded, and he hosted study sessions and parties at his lodging. What I learned from the Sergeant Major is attitudes can change very quickly under the right conditions so don't be so totally fixated with a preset opinion that you lose focus on the present environment. This soldier's experience ended up being much better than he could have ever imagined because he allowed himself to honestly judge the environment around him and change his attitude accordingly.

An interesting thing happened while I was at the academy as I decided to retire at the twenty-year mark which was still a year away. While I was likely going to be promoted during the next promotion cycle, I was facing some big changes. I was going to be moved over to the Security Forces Squadron to be their First Sergeant and would soon be deployed for six months to the Middle East. I was also being capped at one three-year First Sergeant tour and would have to return to a flying assignment. My plane, the

C-141 Starlifter was being retired from service, so I was going to be assigned to a C-17 or C-130 flying billet, which meant several more months of school and six months of consistent flying after that to get upgraded. This meant twelve to fifteen months away from home and another relocation. I was tired of leaving the family and very happy with the stability of being home all the time, so after consulting with Suzan, I decided to apply for retirement. Retiring meant my son James was going to have to attend his senior year of high school in a new state and this would be his third high school in three different states, but it also meant that Brandon would have stability of living in the same location from 8th grade on.

Brandon and I attending a military veteran event at the Arthur Blank Foundation

Suzan was keen on having me home, but she was also very nervous that we would be leaving the only life we had ever known, and on most days we both really loved the Air Force. I submitted the retirement application a full year out, which was a big deal. At this time in the Air Force, this action meant I was prohibited from testing for promotion, changing jobs, or moving locations. Some mentors and leadership tried to talk me out of it, but I decided to forge ahead, and I would use the year to my benefit to figure out how to transition from the military, find a job, and become a civilian.

6
CIVILIAN TRANSITION JOURNEY

In your core you can still be a Soldier, Sailor, Airman, or Marine but at the end of the day you must change that a bit to assimilate into your new role in the private sector. –John Phillips, VETLANTA Co-Founder and Vice President

When I decided to retire, my strategy was to target two very separate tracks. The first was more of a backup plan and that was to become a Junior Reserve Officers' Training Corps (ROTC) Instructor at a high school. My brother John retired and was doing the same thing back in Illinois and was happy with it. I worked very well with high school kids and loved teaching, so I strongly considered the same path. I completed the application process which consisted of a medical evaluation, mental health review, records review, and interview with the local instructor. My application was reviewed, and I had targeted several potential openings in North Carolina, Tennessee, and Texas but decided to focus on the other option and that was to land a position in logistics with a Fortune 500 Company.

During this pursuit, I made bad assumptions about finding civilian employment. The good news is I had a full year left on active duty to figure things out. My first bad assumption was that I was going to have an abundance of resources available to help me out and TAPS would be hugely beneficial. While there are a significant number of resources available today, in 2007 that wasn't the case and TAPS class was subpar. If you are not familiar with TAPS, it stands for Transition Assistance Program and it has outcome-based modular curriculum designed to prepare service members for transitioning into civilian life. To the government's credit, TAPS has been improved, but in 2007 it was not good and ill prepared service members for their transition.

The program was three days long and could be taken any time before separation and up to a full year prior. The three days covered everything transition related including the process, health, wellness, education, benefits, networking, creating a resume, applying, interviewing, and the job offer process. I believe we spent all of a half day on employment and only half of the class was able to do a five-minute mock interview. TAPS was a congressionally mandated program shoved into the bureaucratic system which generated a highly ineffective programs with marginal outputs and probably even fewer positive outcomes.

As I mentioned, there weren't a lot of resources available in 2007 to help with the transition, especially in the nonprofit space, but I'd done a huge amount of reading and research. I subscribed to *GI Jobs* magazine and would read it cover to cover to find out who the veteran friendly employers were and to get advice from veterans who had made the transition successfully. I was honored several years later when they featured me in the magazine.

My next bad assumption was companies would be okay with hiring me six months from retirement. I had no idea that most companies fill their positions within days after advertising and very few companies project future openings that far in advance. I'd started applying way too early and ran into a few roadblocks, but I also landed on the radar of several companies and the job interviews were very good practice. My next bad assumption is I could create a credible and competitive resume using software I bought at Walmart and wouldn't need any outside assistance. Wow, what a train wreck that was. I spent a late evening and early morning gathering all my awards, performance reports, and my "I love me" binder and created what I though was a brilliant resume that would without a doubt land me a job in corporate America.

It turned out to be a resume with flaws that plague veterans' resumes even today. First and foremost is It being seven pages in length, which means most anyone I'd send it to had sent it right to a digital or actual trashcan. The second was I had not translated any of it. It was full of military jargon, acronyms, and it would never be understandable by someone who hadn't been in the Air Force at some point in time in their life. My resume was also not targeted as that concept was new for me. This was a big issue as I was applying for a wide range of jobs in many different specialty areas including aviation, logistics, human resources, and program management. A one size fits all approach with resumes is a farce that will close doors for you. I'm super thankful to a civilian who worked at the Airman and Family Readiness Center at Seymour Johnson who told me very directly that my resume was terrible and that I needed to throw it away and start from scratch. He supplied a nice format and solid advice and the new resume I created instantly produced results. Today, there are many credible nonprofit organizations that will supply resume aid free of charge and I always recommend Hire Heroes USA, which provides free resumes, mock interviews, and career counselling to veterans and spouses.

I interviewed with and received offers from Union Pacific for an operations supervisor position, GE Middle River Aircraft for an employee relations supervisor position, a chicken frying plant for a plant safety manager position, a Kubota dealership for a general manager position, and I turned down all of these offers as they were not good fits for me or were not in a desirable location to live. I was comfortable turning down these offers because I had the Air Force JROTC job as a backup plan, which gave me added flexibility along with the fact that I was still several months away from starting terminal leave and I still had time.

I really wanted to live in the south, work at a corporate office, and work for a very large company. I had applied for several organizations which met *all* these criteria but had received no callbacks until UPS called. I had applied for an Aircraft Load Planning job for UPS Airlines in Charlotte, which appeared to be an attractive fit as I was very qualified, loved load planning, and Charlotte was a very desirable area to live. I received an instant job offer on the very first call, but it was a part-time, twenty hours per week position. I was almost offended with the offer but closed out the call with something meaningful to the HR Supervisor. I told her that I had only worked for two companies in my entire life. One was a job that lasted two months and the other was a career that had lasted twenty years, and I wasn't as interested in obtaining a job as I was looking for my next career. I owe a lot to this diligent supervisor as she went out and found an excellent fit for me at UPS.

I was very interested in working at UPS, but most of their positions are part-time positions and, at the time, they had a very strict promote-from-within culture and management positions were very rarely filled with external candidates. The exception was when they could not find candidates internally with the required skills and experience for the position. The Government Operations Manager job description seemed like it was written specifically with me in mind. They were looking for someone who had security manager experience, who had worked in the past with military and civilian airlift, knew the basics of load planning, had served an assignment at Air Mobility Command or US Transportation Command, and had a college degree in Logistics.

I conducted three phone interviews for this position and during the final phone interview, which was on a Wednesday, I mentioned that I lived just six hours away from Atlanta and had flexibility to come down for an in-person interview at any time. On Thursday at 1:30 PM, I received a call from Suzan, and she advised that there was a message on our answering machine that asked that I come to Atlanta for an in-person interview on Friday at 7:30 AM. My commander gave me a 24-hour pass and I confirmed the interview, finished the workday, rented a car, grabbed my suit bag from the closet and my dress shoes, and made the drive down to Atlanta arriving at 1:00 AM. I woke up extra early to practice interview questions and to ensure I'd found the building and went to put my suit on at 6:15 AM only to have one of the biggest shocks in my life. In my hurry, I'd grabbed the suit bag for my son James! At the time he wrestled in the 132-pound class, and I was kicking about 220 so the pants didn't even fit past my thigh. I had driven down in shorts and a t-shirt, so this suit was the only clothes I had with me. In the next sixty seconds, I cried, I quit, I felt sorry for myself, I got angry, and then I found resolve and determination. I ran to the front counter and scared the poor Indian clerk working behind the counter when, thinking that he might have a suit in the back room, I yelled out "I need a suit and I need it now." His eyes got super big, and he pointed west and stated, "Walmart."

I drove like a banshee to find Walmart and when I entered there were George Suits right at the front of the store. I bought one for about $80 and got dressed in the parking lot and, once again, I drove like a banshee to UPS Supply Chain Corporate

Campus in Alpharetta, Georgia, making it to the parking lot at 7:25 AM where I would be interviewing with an HR Manager and the hiring manager who was a retired Navy F-14 Radar Intercept Officer (think Goose from Top Gun). The interview went very well, but I don't believe they made their minds up to hire me until the very last question they asked. The question was "Tell me about a stressful time where your quick actions and determination made a difference." They were shocked when I started my answer with "Ninety minutes ago . . ." and relayed the story. They laughed and were amazed at the same time. The HR manager advised that I could have interviewed without the suit, and she really liked my reply which was, "Would you have even considered hiring me if I came in here dressed in shorts, flip flops, and a t-shirt because I certainly would not." I wore that George Suit for about seven years until Suzan made me throw it away.

They liked me and instantly arranged for me to take the management exams which took two hours, and I passed all three. There was also a requirement to meet a board of three UPS Managers for a Q&A session, but they were impressed and I received a waiver from the business unit vice president who was an Army veteran. I got home at 10:00 PM, woke up the next day at 5:00 AM to take James to a wrestling tournament then made the drive to Norfolk, Virginia, to attend a two-day Bradley Morris hiring event. I was ecstatic a couple of days later to hear back from the HR manager who informed me they were going to extend a job offer to me.

Several days later I received the job offer and was far from impressed. Even coming in as a manager, I was going to take a significant pay cut and my number of vacation days were going to change from thirty in the military to four for the first year and would be pegged at ten until year five. I was somewhat familiar with the job offer process from all the research I had did, so I decided to counteroffer. I knew they could say no, say yes, pull the offer, counteroffer, or go silent. I was blessed that they decided to counter my offer and while I was still going to take a pay cut, I very naively and arrogantly thought I would get promoted up the chain and make real money in the near future. I'm very thankful to the hiring manager, HR manager, and the leadership for holding the position open for me for two months as I received the offer in February and wouldn't be able to start until I finished my commitment with the Air Force in April.

I was leaving the Air Force after an amazing twenty-year career and the best thing was I was leaving in my own terms, leaving a better person than when I started, and leaving while still in love with the Air Force. It was a remarkable run and, while all my experiences in the Air Force weren't terrific, a majority were, and Suzan and I were so thankful to the friends we made along the way and the memories we made together which will sustain me for a very long time.

7
CORPORATE AMERICA JOURNEY

The more valuable you make your service to others, the more profitable it will be to you. –Jim Casey, UPS Founder

I had my retirement ceremony and party on a Friday and moved to Cumming, Georgia, the next day and started with UPS that Monday. Suzan stayed with the boys until they finished school in mid-June, so I was on my own for ten weeks to close on the house, get settled in, and start at UPS. That Monday, I nervously got dressed to start my first day at UPS Supply Chain Solutions as a Government Tender Manager. For those of you who weren't in the military you might not fully appreciate the nervousness about getting dressed. In the military we are told every day exactly what to wear and while there might be some combinations available, we essentially don't have to worry about matching or looking trendy. Military instructions also supply very specific dress and appearance guidelines, so we know what our uniforms are supposed to look like and the standards for haircuts and grooming. I went to work that morning just scared out of my mind that I looked like a total goober and UPS would send me packing after just one day.

My first week at UPS was interesting. I received about fifteen minutes of onboarding information and was handed over to the manager who hired me who had traveled down to Atlanta from Dayton, Ohio, for my first week. During that week, he provided without about twenty-five minutes of direction, introduced me to two people, and told me to go figure it out.

The group I would be working in was a new group and I would play a very big part in consolidating old groups and setting things up at our corporate campus in Alpharetta. I was working for our freight forwarding arm and not the traditional brown small-package side of the house. My going joke when asked if I've ever delivered packages is "I'm not anywhere near cool enough to wear those brown shorts and socks." The freight forwarding group at UPS was created out of several acquisitions including Menlo Worldwide Forwarding and Fritz. Menlo Worldwide forwarding at one point in time was Emery Worldwide and included an airline, however the company lost their FAA Air Certificate after a crash in 2000 and a mechanical incident a year later.

If you are not aware of what a freight forwarding group is, the folks at Indeed.Com offer a nice explanation:

> A freight forwarder is a company that serves as an intermediary between transportation companies that import and export goods and the businesses that need them. Freight forwarders manage every aspect of the transportation process, from storing goods before shipment to ensuring they make it through customs. They don't handle the movement of the goods themselves, but they establish relationships with the companies that do so they can plan each step of every shipment on a client's behalf. Freight forwarders work with transportation companies that ship products by road, rail, water, and air.

Essentially, we purchase space on planes, trains, trucks, and ships to handle shipping requirements for customers. The business is highly competitive as there are tens of thousands of freight forwarders ranging from one employee to bigger companies like UPS, which has tens of thousands of freight forwarding employees. It's a bit more complex at UPS because we do own some assets like trucks and buildings, and we can use UPS Airlines aircraft when there is space available.

The government group from Menlo had largely been disbanded and now consisted of a small office in Harrisburg, Pennsylvania, with four employees and a dedicated government sales office in Chantilly, Virginia, near to Dulles Airport, which was being closed. My first two tasks were to head up the Harrisburg office to introduce myself and then drive down to Chantilly to close that office. The folks in Harrisburg were tough and untrusting of UPS but understood that I was new and from the outside so they really gave me the benefit of the doubt which a seasoned UPSer would probably not have gotten. They also provided me with details on exactly what government business we had and graciously explained the difference between a government contract and a tender.

Chantilly was a much different story. When I arrived, there were only two administrative assistants left as the other twelve plus employees had already been laid off. These two were offered positions in Alpharetta but that was not possible for them, and both were bitter about losing their jobs. One was a younger employee who was several years out of college. He would have been my assistant if he had accepted the job, and to his credit, he sucked it up and conducted a full four days of training providing me with very specific details on what my job was and how to do it. The other assistant was less than gracious and spent four days reprimanding me. She yelled at me for taking two new UPS coffee cups out of the trash to bring back to the team in Georgia. I sucked it up and decided it would not be in my or her best interest to go "First Sergeant" on her and instead show her grace and empathy for what she was going through. I ended up working with her several years later as she went to work for a vendor we used, and she was sweet to me for years even when I ended the contract with her employer.

One of my tasks at this location was to decide what documents needed to be kept and shipped to my office, put in permanent storage, or be destroyed. The crazy thing is Menlo had a unique culture where they printed everything, so each of the twelve offices had over thirty large binders in additional to file cabinets, which were stuffed full to the brim with documents. This was super uncomfortable because I had only worked at UPS for two weeks and had absolutely no idea what I was looking at. I ended up saving about ten boxes worth of documents to be permanently stored, about ten boxes to be shipped to my office, and about fifty boxes to be shredded. I called my boss up to let him know that I would be there for a month if I had to use the office shredder and he directed me to hire a company to have the items picked up and shredded, which I promptly did.

On the day this was supposed to happen, I showed up in the morning and all the boxes of documents to be shredded were gone. I asked the assistant if the shredding company showed up early and she said the janitor had taken everything to the dumpster on the previous night and the trash truck had already come that morning. I was very upset as I believed I would be promptly fired. Some of you probably would not have said anything, but I've witnessed in my Air Force career multiple times that covering up a mistake with a lie is a sin that just makes things a lot worse in the end. While it wasn't directly my mistake, the situation was under my control and therefore I was going to accept responsibility. I called my manager, explained the situation and he said that it was okay, as these documents no longer had any valuable or sensitive information. I believe he was impressed with my integrity and the fact that I had gotten the job done.

I returned home and started figuring out the job which was not overly complicated once you figured out the process, procedures, and contacts. My job consisted of managing fifty domestic air tenders. These tenders were pricing sheets to be used by military customers when they needed to move cargo within the lower forty-eight states by air. We had a dozen account managers who would visit the military customers and they in turn would inform me if the rates were too low or too high. I would access a U.S. Government system and change the rates and publish the new tenders in their system, implement the new rates with UPS pricing, and inform the wider sales group of the rate change. Within weeks, I could do the job in my sleep and became bored very quickly.

The culture at the time was very different from the Air Force. UPS is a very socially responsible company, but we are far from being social butterflies, especially in my building which seats about 1,500 employees. It can be strangely quiet at times. When I first arrived, I would walk down the hallway and wish people a good morning and I would often not get a reply. It made me angry but I recalled that for several years I'd done the same thing when someone wished me good morning and I was so busy and stressed that I didn't say anything back before I figured out what I had done and chased the person down the hallway to apologize. During that first year no one really went out of their way to mentor me or make me feel welcome outside of an Air Force Reserve Captain who had been hired at the same time. I was also advised several times to concentrate solely on my assigned duties and not swim outside of my lane, which means I shouldn't look for additional work.

I was so bored that I would buy the *Atlanta Journal Constitution* and *USA Today* and read them cover to cover each morning and I purchased a membership for the gym across the street and used to take a daily ninety-minute lunch/gym breaks. At about the six-month point, I was very discouraged and ready to leave and gave my direct manager an ultimatum. They either needed to give me added responsibility with a promotion or I was going to walk. I was blessed that they came back with a promotion and a significant opportunity that would go on to supply huge value to UPS and serve me well.

While we were solid at the government domestic tender business, we were pathetic with the transactional business, which are called one-day quotes. These are opportunities to handle a shipment which is currently ready to move and there is no contractual pricing available for several reasons. It could be to a location where standard pricing isn't available or it could be a commodity that needed a special aircraft or special routing. Menlo had a dedicated government desk prior to the acquisitions, and they had enough continuity to be somewhat decent at it. When UPS bought Menlo, they combined all the specialized customer services desks and worked well with the other sectors but wrecked any chance at winning this type of transactional government business.

Military customers hated our approach as it was full of call center rules. The call centers operated from a script, and they were really limited on what aid they could provide. Sometimes, the customers would not get rates until weeks later and these rates were often not be in the same ballpark as our competitors. We were winning at best one percent of opportunities and making just tens of thousands of dollars in revenue each year. I was given the promotion and told to hire two specialist employees and start a dedicated government quote desk at my office. That was the full and only direction I received, which was good and bad.

It was bad as I was so far out of my element and had received no coaching or much support, but it was good as I could be creative and would not be micromanaged and wouldn't be pushed into the "we've always done it this way" paradigm. At the same time, I was standing up this customer service desk, I had a run in with one of those big banks that would help me decide how I wanted the team to operate. Suzan and I had bought new living room furniture and while I despise financing anything, I couldn't really pass up one of those three-years-same-as-cash deals. I hate owing anyone anything, so I started making double and triple payments each month. During this time, I made my first international trip for UPS to Dubai and when I had returned, I had a bill in the mail that included a late fee and a twenty percent finance charge and, even though I was eight payments ahead, I had missed a payment during the trip. It took me a day and a half to figure out the phone number to call and the exact number sequence I needed to dial to talk to a live human being. I will never forget that it was a total of twenty-seven keystrokes on the phone to talk to a rep, which was ludicrous. I set about creating a customer service desk as if I was the customer. I wanted our military customers to be able to speak to a rep without going through a phone menu and to keep this a small, dedicated, and specialized team who could establish relationships with our customers.

When I started setting up the group, I received call center procedures which advised that I should create a phone menu in order to direct customers to a website and a bunch of other rules including scripts, a strict limit of three quotes per call, a fifteen-minute time limit for all calls, and a statistics package where I could review phone statistics for each of my specialists to ensure they were efficient on each call and to ensure they were handling the maximum number of calls per shift. While this might work for most customers, it was not going to work for the military tender business, which is complex and requires significant coordination and specific knowledge to be successful.

I hired two specialists from outside of UPS and onboarded them. We then sat in a small conference room in my building and figured out how to complete quotes and created a very rudimentary template on Excel, which we would fill in by hand for each quote request. This was super simple and much different from what had been done in the past, however it was the right solution for that time and that customer base. I trained the two specialists, who were not veterans, on the basics of the military including ranks, base locations, branches of service, and got them up to speed on the wars in Iraq and Afghanistan.

In just thirty days from hiring the two specialists, we activated the tollfree line and started fielding calls. We had zero marketing support and no advertising, so our success would depend on word of mouth, which meant we were going to have to be very good, very early. It was stressful as the three of us sat in a cubicle together waiting for the phone to ring for the first time as we all had a lot riding on this, maybe even our jobs.

When the phone rang for the first time, there was a big sigh of shared relief and off to work we went. The first quote solution would have never been plausible under the old system as it was complex. It was a quote for a military customer looking to ship 100 mattresses to the war zone in Iraq. We broke all the past call center rules as it took a full day with dozens of long-distance calls to coordinate the rates and to figure out if it was operationally feasible. While we didn't win this opportunity, we turned heads as we were able to come up with a solution with competitive rates in a short time and additional opportunities would quickly follow.

In that first month we quadrupled the revenue secured for the previous year for government quotes, and by month five, I was given the authorization to hire an additional resource to the team and filled it with an Air Force veteran. Two of the three original specialists are still at UPS fifteen years later with one working in corporate compliance as a supervisor and the other working as a product supervisor. Just a year later this team would grow to five specialists and a supervisor, and soon we had our first million-dollar month. We were winning at such high percentages that I received a visit from the vice president who oversaw our centralized customer service center as she wanted to know my "secret sauce." The funny thing is when she visited, she brought the call center script and standard operating procedures to the meeting, and when she asked about my "secret sauce," I picked up both documents and threw them in the trash and said, "that's my secret." She wasn't very impressed and didn't see my solution as something that could be cost-effective at a larger scale, but it didn't slow our group down. Just a year later, I was asked to establish a commercial quote team to support large commercial customers.

My career at UPS would end up being something very different and challenging and I'll compare it to my time coaching little league sports. As I mentioned, I was a wrestler in high school and during my assignment at Wright-Patterson Air Force Base, I volunteered to start a little league wrestling club on the base for kindergarten through sixth grade kids. I did this for two years and we went on to be super successful and we had fun doing it. My wrestling parents were amazing and stayed out of my hair largely because most of them knew very little about wrestling. That was so much fun that I decided to coach little league baseball. This turned out to be a completely different experience as every dad thought they were Pete Rose or Johnny Bench and micromanaged every decision I made, which was crazy since this was a coach pitch league that didn't keep score.

This was very similar to the two customer support teams as everyone stayed out of my hair with the government business because they didn't know it but micromanaged me on the commercial business. To be honest, when someone tried to micromanage me on the government business, I would just throw a bunch of military acronyms and jargon at them and say something like this "The tender in GFM needs to be modified, so I need to call up SDDC to get guidance but they will probably refer me to USTRANSCOM to fix the RDD issue, but since it will require a policy change and it's for the CENTCOM theater I will have to engage with AMC A3 and CENTCOM AMD." I would usually get a blank stare followed by, "Let me know how that goes." Both desks are still active fifteen years later and collectively have made several hundred million dollars of revenue since they were created.

During this period my boss, the Navy officer who hired me, decided to leave UPS as he became frustrated on not being promoted. When he left, I was promoted into his position which was my second promotion in my first eighteen months at UPS. I learned a valuable lesson during this time that burnout was real. I had not taken a real vacation during my last two years in the Air Force to save days for my terminal leave when I retired and since vacation days were pro-rated for my first year at UPS, I had not taken a vacation during year one. I had saved up most of my ten vacation days to take at the end of year two during the holidays. When I received this promotion, I was now the manager overseeing government operations and had to fire a manager in early December. I ended up doing my new job and his for the entire month of December, and as a result, going into year three at UPS, I was totally burned out and struggling mentally and physically.

This burnout along with this next story reinforced the importance of taking real vacations and it changed my life for the better going forward. Our UPS Freight Forwarding Operations Manager in Hawaii was an Army veteran and someone I grew close to over the years. During his several decades of being in the logistics business in Hawaii, he'd formed solid relationships with the military throughout the islands and was super passionate about supporting the troops and would often bend the rules, which at times became a real thorn in my side because I was responsible for compliance in the government sector. Even with that, we became good friends, and I had the pleasure of spending a full week with him twice during customer visits to Hawaii.

During the second visit, he mentioned that Tahiti and Fiji were on his bucket list, and he would take a vacation to those locations when he retired down the road. The facts are that he had the vacation time and the money to go and was in a perfect staging area to travel to both countries, but he was too concerned about being away from the job with limited connectivity for a two-week period as he thought he was too important for the business. Unfortunately, he passed away from cancer prior to retiring and didn't fulfill these bucket list items. What I learned from this story and the burnout was you must take care of yourself. Most companies will talk a big game about work-life balance, but if you don't control that balance, it's probably not going to happen. We all missed him when he passed away, but the business went on.

I learned life is to short not to take advantage of those bucket list opportunities especially if you have the resources. While living without Suzan is hard, I take comfort in knowing that we checked off many of our bucket list items including traveling to Rome, London, Salzburg, Athens, Aruba, Antigua, Grand Cayman, Kuai, Jamacia, St. Lucia, Bahamas, and Puerto

Rico just to name a few. The memories we made during these trips sustain me today and often bring smiles when I see the pictures pop up on my iPhone.

The next lesson I learned almost cost me my job, but it also kicked my career into overdrive, and I learned incredible lessons. It was time for one of our biggest government contracts to be re-bid, which meant we had to create a formal response document for the government which would provide an overview of our capabilities, our operations plan, pricing, and details on our safety and compliance plan. The response would be twenty pages of information and another five pages of pricing. One of my good friends and now a former UPS colleague Neil Dursley, a British citizen who managed UPS Freight Forwarding Operations in the Middle East, was given responsibility of creating the response document. He knew the business better than anyone else, however he was also completely overwhelmed and didn't have much time to take on a project like this. After watching zero activity for weeks and seeing a quickly approaching deadline, I volunteered to create the response although I had almost zero assistance and even less experience.

I spent two weeks researching, collecting data and information, and translating the data and information into the twenty pages of verbiage. I used every bit of the two weeks, including the weekends, to put this response together and wrapped it up the night before the proposal was due because of issues with getting rates back from our pricing group. On the morning the submission was due, I got up very early and made it to the office by 7:00 AM to email the document to TRANSCOM, which is the higher headquarters that oversees air, ocean, sea, road, and rail transport for the military.

Several minutes after sending the email, I received a phone call from the contracting officer who was a civilian who I'd been stationed with when we were both active-duty airmen at HQ Air Mobility Command at Scott Air Force Base just several years earlier. He informed me that email submissions were not being accepted and I would have to hand deliver the document with a wet ink signature and the deadline was just six hours away and no extensions would be granted. The next sixty seconds reminded me of the suit debacle, but I quickly came up with a game plan and executed it. I grabbed the original response with the wet ink signature, shoved it into a large brown envelope, hopped in my truck and made flight reservations to St. Louis on my drive to Atlanta's Hartsfield Jackson Airport. While it wasn't ideal, I was going to have ninety minutes to spare, until Mother Nature stepped in. A large snowstorm was passing through St. Louis, and we ended up circling over the airport for about an hour. When I arrived, I rented a car and made the slow and treacherous twenty-five-mile drive from the airport to Scott Air Force Base in the snow and ice. I arrived on the base, parked the car, and sprinted into the building with just five minutes to spare.

The contracting officer, who had zero personality and less empathy, showed up in the lobby, pulled our proposal, and used a ruler to measure every spreadsheet of the five pages of pricing and the only thing he said was I was very lucky that I had not resized any of the cells and said I could stay in the lobby until I caught my breath. I ended up getting back home around midnight, exhausted but relieved that I had not totally screwed up our opportunity to win this contract, but I was very wrong.

About three weeks later, we received an email stating that our submission was rejected, and we would be eliminated from contention which at the time had been around forty million dollars of revenue each year for my company. The slap in the face from the government was our proposal was rejected for a totally bureaucratic reason. When filling out the header of the twenty-page response, I listed the company name as UPS and not the name UPS Airlines, and since you had to be an airline to submit a proposal we were thrown out of contention. Upon receiving the rejection, we pleaded our case with the contracting officer only to be rejected again. It took going up to very high levels at UPS, several lawyers, and going to very high levels at TRANSCOM for them to reverse their decision. I got metaphorically punched in the face by a lot of different leaders at UPS for this mistake but most realized that we would have never submitted a proposal if it weren't for me and, when we won the contract, all was forgiven and I was given assurances of additional support going forward.

The lessons I learned are still valid today. Just because you volunteer for something, doesn't mean you won't be held accountable if it doesn't go well. Attention to detail is incredibly important, especially in contracting, and you need to ensure you know and understand what the exact requirements are. The next lesson is to ask for help when you need it. If we didn't win the contract, I would have probably been fired because I hadn't asked for assistance. Lastly, I learned that there are going to be jerks in this world who you are going to have to encounter, so don't give them any sort of benefit of the doubt or any reason to hang you out to dry.

After we won it, I picked up the additional responsibility to oversee the operations of this contract even though it did not have a U.S. geographic operational component as its origins and destinations were all in the Middle East, Afghanistan, and Northern Africa. I ended up making some tweaks to our operations and aligned with a solid charter broker company and we substantially increased our revenue. My British co-worker in Dubai was selected to move to the United States and take on a newly established role as Director of Global Government Operations and would be my manager. After his second visit to Atlanta, I dropped him off at the airport for his return trip back to Dubai and out of gut instinct asked him if I was going to see him again. He quit the very next week. While we never worked together again, we remained friends and I see him from time to time. Within a month of his departure, I was promoted to the role he was supposed to fill. This was my third promotion in my first four years and with this promotion I would start earning real compensation but it came serious stress.

Over the next ten years, my responsibilities would significantly increase. I was able to give up the commercial quote team but accepted responsibility for global government operations including teams in the US, Kuwait, Dubai, Germany and third-party contractors in Qatar, Afghanistan, and Iraq. I would also be responsible for several additional government contracts that were worth several hundred million dollars to UPS annually and added additional clients to the government quote team including all government agencies, humanitarian, oil and gas, and special projects. I was able to hire additional personnel and when the second Gulf War ended, our revenue dropped to zero overnight for Iraq, but we were in a good situation as we were able to quickly pivot to Afghanistan and continued to grow the business.

One of my favorite sayings is "Success breeds more work" and this was so true as I inherited even more responsibility, including oversight of the oil and gas team in Houston, an internal operations response group in Louisville, and a commercial retail product team with employees in Chicago, Los Angeles, and Alpharetta. There is a saying at UPS which is "No manager at UPS will ever be comfortable with a job as when they get comfortable, more responsibility will be added to keep them uncomfortable" and wow, that was so true for my first thirteen years.

In my role as Director of Global Government Operations, I was able to travel to Afghanistan and become just the third

UPS employee to visit. UPS had had a presence in Afghanistan since December 2001 through the freight forwarding company we purchased, however our engagement was limited to third-party contractors and assets. We were not allowed to send UPS employees or UPS aircraft to the war zones, nor could we have our logos present on signage or uniforms. I was able to lobby hard and get the logo rule eliminated and changed the employee policy to allow visits by senior leadership. I'd never made it to Afghanistan during my Air Force career, but I visited our operations several times at Kandahar Air Base, Camp Leatherneck, and Bagram Air Base. I'm very proud of these visits not because of any sort of bravery but because I made a difference with the people who worked on our business.

Our agent's employees in Afghanistan were a mix of hippies, adventure seekers, and people looking to improve their living standards from the United States, Canada, Hungary, Philippines, India, and Nigeria. The pay was outstanding, especially in the early years, but the danger was real and living conditions were challenging. We had offices set up at four locations in Afghanistan and our agent's employees lived on the base in small compounds. These compounds were comprised of office space, living quarters, cargo staging yards, and space for the equipment like vehicles, forklifts, and generators. *Living quarters* is a term I use loosely as the personnel lived two people per room in converted twenty-foot ocean cargo containers, which had electricity to power lights, heating, and air-conditioning. The containers had two single beds, two footlockers, two nightstands and two chairs per room. Latrine service was better than what our troops had in combat but weren't great. Each compound had one or two showers and sinks shared by dozens of personnel.

Chow was amazing for most of the time as the agents had access to the military dining facilities which were remarkable.

But the military, in its finest red-tape bureaucracy, would later change this policy and make contractors pay for meals though, admittedly, they didn't have a system to accept payment in Afghanistan, which essentially cut off dining facility access to hundreds of contractors on the U.S. military bases throughout Afghanistan. I'll never forget the response from a civilian contracting specialist when I asked her how we should feed our people and she informed me they could eat at Burger King since it was open 24/7 on the bases. Clearly, she had never deployed a day in her life, nor had she ever been responsible for the health, safety, or wellness of personnel in a deployed environment. Our contractor ended up building kitchens in their compounds and secured groceries from multiple sources. Even with these rough living conditions, many of these third-party contractors worked in Afghanistan for seven+ years and I relate it to being institutionalized as they received a place to live, three square meals a day, and direction on what to do 24/7.

When I decided to make my first visit to Afghanistan, Suzan asked me who was ordering me to go, and I had to admit that I had decided to go on my own accord. She was upset and worried, but I explained that I had an obligation to the 100 contractor workers and seeing our operations firsthand would allow me to better manage the business. I flew to Dubai, spent a week visiting customers and clients, and met up with Norris El-Hiraki who today is still a very good friend I refer to as the "Tennesyrian" because his mom is from Tennessee and his dad is Syrian. Norris grew up in the Middle East and had worked for FedEx in Dubai until we hired him as our Government Operations Manager for the Middle East.

Hanging out with the Tennesyrian during a business trip to Los Angles

Norris had been to Afghanistan multiple times with FedEx and was UPS employee number two to go in country. We made the trip to Afghanistan together on a Sunday morning which was pleasant and didn't seem at all dangerous as it was a commercial Fly Dubai Boeing 737 flight, which would land directly on Kandahar Air Base. This was much different than any combat deployments I had in the past as I was dressed in Khakis without any body armor or weapon. I had explained to Suzan that I wouldn't need any of this protection as I would always be on the military base and not in any direct danger.

Our compound on Kandahar was very elaborate and the best living conditions of any of our compounds in Afghanistan. It was constructed with a total of twenty-four, forty-foot ocean containers, which had been connected via interior and exterior corridors. It almost looked like a Swiss chalet. It had a small shelter off to the side which was made up of sandbags and concrete, which would provide protection from any small arms fire or shrapnel from mortars. While the compound was fairly comfortable, it was directly adjacent to what was known as the "poo pond." This pond was legendary with even the *New York Times* dedicating an article to it. The poo pond was an open sewer pit for all the human waste for the base, which was substantial since there were over 20,000 personnel living and working on the installation. Our compound was so close to it that everything smelled like human excrement including the people, paperwork, vehicles, bedding, furniture, and anything else in the compound.

Within an hour of arriving, the base warning siren went off indicating an imminent attack and multiple mortars were launched by Taliban terrorists from the city directly outside of the base. My military training snapped into play, and I quickly moved to the shelter where I sat with six Nigerian subcontractors and waited for a half hour until all clear signal was given. The crazy "Tennesyrian" spent the whole time on the second-floor balcony of the building, smoking a cigar and yelling at me to come see the fireworks. I probably should have counseled him, but I guarantee no HR employee at UPS would ever believe what they read. That night, the wind direction shifted, and we received the full brunt of the poo pond and both of us were woken out of a dead sleep at 2:30 AM.

We got up and took a short and pleasant flight from Kandahar Air Base to Bagram Air Base where we faced almost polar opposite conditions. The base was very safe, and I was even able to go on an evening stroll by myself and grab a cup of coffee at Green Bean Coffee Company, which was a vendor for the Army Air Force Exchange Service and had coffee shops on several installations in Afghanistan. The food at the dining halls was made by Afghan contractors working on the base, and it was incredible. To this day, it is some of the best barbecue I've ever had.

Living and working conditions for our subcontractor employees had a lot to be desired. When I arrived, I was told they didn't have a place for me to sleep in our compound but, not to worry, as one of our competitors had a compound next door and a bed was available in the general manager's room. I found out the GM was the manager I'd fired several years prior and politely told our GM that I have an unwritten rule, which is to never sleep in the same room in a war zone with an employee I've fired. I grabbed a pillow and a blanket and slept on the office floor for two nights, which was much better than our "poo pond" lodging at Kandahar.

The real reason they tried to put me in outside quarters was our compound was in terrible condition. The offices and living quarters were beyond dirty and the bathroom was in terrible working order with just one sink and one shower operable for over twenty people. When I questioned the GM, he said they were extremely short-staffed and working missions around the clock and he didn't have the staffing available to properly clean and repair the camp. During the next twenty-four hours, I was able to spend good quality time with the contractor employees and visited several Army and Air Force customers. The next day, we hopped on a plane headed and headed for Camp Leatherneck. This was a large 1,600-acre base that was used by the US Marine Corps and was the main operating base for the British military in Afghanistan. The flight was uneventful but a little nerve wracking as it was on a very small propeller aircraft. Norris and I were the only passengers, and we were flying over a desolate and barren land that looked like the surface of the moon.

This was our newest operating location in Afghanistan, the most remote, and was getting consistently busy. The amount of air freight moving through this location was inspiring given the staff was so small. The offices and living quarters were made up of eight twenty-foot cargo containers but the GM ran a very tight ship at this location. The facilities were clean and in good working order and he even put a mint on our pillows that night. What they were missing was equipment and simply didn't have enough vehicles and mission support equipment to effectively service the mission or grow the business. We visited several Marine Corps customers and afterwards that night ended up being one of my best memories traveling for UPS as we sat outside around a firepit as Norris and I visited with the team.

The next day I flew back to Dubai and immediately upon landing, called one of the owners and senior leaders of our subcontractor and directed him to meet me for dinner. We had a nice dinner and I laid it out for him. They needed to increase staffing at Bagram and get the living and working conditions to standard and send the additional equipment to Camp Leatherneck and he needed to consider this a mandate and not a recommendation. To their credit they jumped on it, and a month later I received a call from the GM at Bagram who was extremely thankful. I have nothing but huge respect for our subcontractor employees who worked in Afghanistan. While they had different motives than those who served in the American Military in Afghanistan, they raised their hands to go over there to better their lives and the lives of their families and most served the U.S. military business with great pride.

8
CHANGING THE CULTURE JOURNEY

Culture is not an initiative. Culture is the enabler of all initiatives. –Larry Senn, Author and "Father of Corporate Culture"

When I first arrived at UPS, I was in for a significant culture shock. I came from a culture in the Air Force that made available consistent volunteer opportunities and ample leadership development. UPS, at least in my corporate campus, did align several volunteer roles with leadership development but most volunteerism was limited to United Way season, which was about a month in the fall. As for formal leadership *self*-development, the only notable available options to the masses were Toastmasters and Women's Leadership Development (WLD). I didn't require assistance with public speaking but became involved with United Way as a volunteer and with WLD as a participant and supporter.

One of my first successes on the volunteer front is I started an International Food Day on which employees made food items from different regions across the globe, which we would sell with all proceeds to go to United Way. This ended up being a huge hit as our workforce is very diverse with employees from across the world and we would have over fifty tables set up which would raise several thousand dollars. Fifteen years later, this event is still going strong, but it has been taken over by our IT group and when I tell people I started the event, they don't believe me.

UPS was decades ahead of establishing Women's Leadership Development and we have chapters at most major facilities across the world. At my location, WLD is very inclusive, and everyone is welcome to attend their lunch and learn events, most of their workshops, and their public speaker series which I took advantage of during my early years at UPS. I did wear out my HR department for years complaining that there needed to be formal leadership development groups for men as well. Several years later, they called me to inform that we were starting Business Resource Groups and asked me if I wanted to start the first Veterans Business Resource Group at UPS.

My first thought was *no way* as I was on the road so much that Suzan complained that she saw more of me when I was a crewmember in the Air Force. I was also rapidly growing my responsibility at work and finishing a master's degree, so my plate had no room on it. Jordan Kellett, one of the two Coast Guardsmen I hired as a Government Operations Specialist wanted to be the co-chair, but the rules required a manager had to be the chair. One of my Air Force Education With Industry Officers pulled me aside and told me this is an opportunity that I shouldn't pass up and if I wasn't going to do it for myself, I should do it for Jordan, so I raised my hand and volunteered.

A Business Resource Group (BRG) is a voluntary, employee-led group that fosters a diverse and inclusive workplace through both internal and external engagement. These groups are normally organized around a particular shared background, interest, or culture and at UPS include veterans, single working parents, Latino, African American, and LBGTQA groups to name a few. These groups are also known by other names in different companies including affinity groups and networks. When I volunteered to start the first Veterans Business Resource Group (VBRG) we had no budget, no direction, and our company didn't even know which employees were military veterans.

That issue gave us a starting point and our HR department surveyed the entire workforce in the U.S. to see how many employees would self-identify and changed the hiring process to start documenting employees with military service. I was shocked when I received the names of the veterans in my building as there were people on the list who I had known for years who I didn't know were veterans. My military service pride is always visible from the veteran plates on my car to the military memorabilia on my desk and even routinely a part of my introduction when I met new people for the first time.

I started going from cubicle to cubicle to introduce myself and let folks know about the VBRG. Several employees who'd had military service during and shortly after the Vietnam War advised they had purposedly kept their military service on the down low as being a veteran during that time was not cool in everyone's eyes. That really gave me motivation as I wanted to recognize veterans from all eras who worked at the company. At our corporate offices, we started putting small flags on each veteran's cube for Veterans Day and had the vice president of each business unit send handwritten thank you cards. I also started a flag raising ceremony at my corporate campus where we had Guard or Reserve employees in their military uniforms or a high school JROTC honor guard or a college ROTC honor guard come out and conduct a flag ceremony.

The first year we did this we had fifty employees show up at 7:30 AM, the second year was 100, and by the third year we had 200 and our president would show to give a speech. This ceremony is now held at multiple UPS buildings across the country each Veterans Day and our CEO normally speaks at the event at our corporate office in Atlanta. We've also sent service pins to each of our 20,000+ veteran employees across the country each year. Our corporate communications department also listened to our feedback and every Veterans Day for two weeks, they run a series of articles about our military veteran workforce and how the company supports veterans. These are all small things, but collectively these small things helped me change the culture in a company that has been around for over 100 years and has over five hundred thousand employees.

Getting ready of the Veterans Day Flag Ceremony at UPS in 2015

One of my favorite stories is how I started the coin tradition at UPS. If you have ever been in the military, you know all about military coins. If you have not, each unit in the military has a unit coin which normally has their unit logo on one side and a variety of other graphics on the other side. Normally everyone who is assigned to that unit will get a unit coin. Certain leadership positions like commanders and First Sergeants will also have personal coins, which they will hand out to troops who have done a good job on something. Traditionally when you hand someone a coin, you put it in your palm and shake the persons hand and give them the coin along with positive words of recognition or encouragement. Coins can also be used to market products or as recognition for events.

The second part of a coin deals with what we in the military call a coin challenge. In the Air Force you would keep your unit coin on you at all times in case you were coin challenged. Anyone with a coin can challenge everyone at a table or in a room by dropping their coin onto a table. When that happens, everyone in the room who is in the military has fifteen seconds to produce their coin by dropping it on the table and, if you don't, you must purchase a round of drinks. The kicker is if you are the challenger, and everyone has a coin, then you must buy the first round. I've been coin checked in the shower, in the bathroom, waiting in line at the dining facility, and everywhere in between. The one rule was you could not coin check anyone on the airplane or on the flight line.

When I significantly grew the government business revenue, leadership gave me a budget and we were able to spend money marketing the government quote team. We purchased nice collateral, coffee mugs, and maps but without a doubt the most valued item was our coin and we produced several different versions. The first version was the VIP and recognition coin, which had UPS on one side and the logos of each branch of service on the other. The second coin was used for marketing, and it had the UPS logo on one side and the name, email address, and toll-free number of the government desk on the other. Getting the coin produced was an adventure in bureaucracy.

Our government marketing team had contacted me for help with the coin and I gave them some design ideas and the name and websites for several companies to purchase them. They readily agreed on the design and manufacturer and then we were hit by internal bureaucracy. Our sales vice president had ideas on what the coin should look like, and we also had to use an approved UPS vendor. Several months later the coins arrived, and it was a train wreck. The coins had been reduced in size by about 40 percent so they could fit in a small replica UPS envelope which had the history of UPS written on it. Our sales leadership thought this was more attractive and would be better for advertising.

What they didn't understand was the military culture. Everyone in the military knew what a coin was and how to hand it over. We had to hand these silly little envelopes over and no one could figure out what we were giving them. It reminded me of handing a Japanese executive my business card. Most of the folks on the receiving end thought it was chocolate or mints inside the envelope and were underwhelmed when they pulled out this little coin. It was awkward at best and embarrassing at worst. To mitigate the silliness and embarrassment, I pulled all the coins out of the envelopes, threw the envelopes away, and handed out the coins the traditional way.

Several months later, while attending the largest annual military transportation conference, five of our government account managers were sitting around a table before the conference discarding the envelopes and had a huge pile of trash at the center of the table that was at least three feet high. Their vice president, the same one who directed the coins be smaller and put in an envelope walked by and lost his mind. He wanted to know why on earth they were discarding something that had been so carefully planned and coordinated to get the highest results from our customers and they threw me under the bus and said it was my idea. Of course, I took full ownership when confronted.

Then, a defining moment happened. This vice president was invited the next day to visit the four-star general at his office on Scott Air Force Base. Most generals in the military will prominently display their coins in their office and this general had an impressive collection including coins from industry partners. When this general would receive a visitor, his executive officer would ensure the coin from that person's organization would be prominently displayed front and center. When our vice president walked in the office, he saw the tiny UPS coin outside of its envelope on a coin rack and it was about half the size of all the other coins in the same rack. The next day new coins were ordered with my design, and they are still floating around the company today.

I learned a valuable lesson during this humorous episode. The vice president had good intentions, but he did not consider the culture and traditions of the customer which he wasn't familiar with, and both are important especially with the United States military. I should have also done a better job explaining the culture and traditions when I recommended that we produce a coin. A year later, I received a call from UPS corporate communications, and they requested I come to our corporate headquarters in Atlanta to teach our CEO how to present a coin as we had a military general visiting later that day. It was special to see the culture change around the company as we came more veteran friendly.

I served two one-year terms as VBRG President, and we implemented several new programs including a speaker series where we would have prominent guest military veterans come speak at our corporate campuses. We had authors, a retired four-star general and Navy SEAL and star of *Ultimate Survival Alaska,* Jared Ogden, speak. The second program was a lunch and learn where we had a UPS subject matter experts come in at lunch and lecture on a wide range of topics including public speaking, developing a brand, writing a book, and networking.

Suzan with Navy SEAL and star of *Ultimate Survival,* Jared Ogden, during a UPS VBRG Event in 2015

My proudest effort as the UPS VBRG President was our partnership with American Corporate Partners (ACP) which is a national nonprofit organization focused on helping returning veterans and active-duty spouses find their next careers through one-on-one mentoring, networking, and online career advice. They were founded by a Wall Street executive in 2008 with the help of six founding corporate partners who provided funding to ACP and volunteer mentors. Currently, ACP has more than 4,000 veterans and active-duty spouses paired one-on-one with mentors from more than 100 of America's top companies, universities, and healthcare systems.

In Atlanta, UPS joined GE, AT&T, and Home Depot as ACP partner companies. In addition to supplying mentors, our four companies would host quarterly panel discussions where past ACP mentees could receive advice and information from veteran professionals in our companies. The first time UPS hosted one of these events, it was organized by the same group of folks who oversaw the UPS coin debacle. Their intent and heart were in the right place however their execution was poor as again they didn't understand the complexities of military transitions.

The evening consisted of a very nice social hour with networking however there were only several UPS military veterans invited and while connections in networking are very valuable, receiving advice from veterans who successfully made the transition from the military to a Fortune 500 company is invaluable, so that was a missed opportunity. After the social hour there was a Q&A session with one of our consultants who was a retired four-star general. The questions from the audience did not go well at all as the transition for a four-star general and non-commissioned and junior officer isn't anywhere in the same stratosphere. The first question asked by a veteran in the crowd was "General, what resources did you use to help you write your resume" and he replied back, "I've never written a resume." The next question was "General, how were you able to find the amazing jobs you have, and his answer was "I sent them my biography." While this event was a missed opportunity, those running it realized that it shouldn't be marketing and sales led, and they handed future ACP events over to the VBRG.

Jordan and I were very enthusiastic about employment and helping transitioning veterans and we jumped into creating events that provided the right value at the right time for the right people at the right place. The right value is conducting events that were beneficial for the time and effort that the mentees, mentors, hosts, and volunteers were putting forth. The right people and right time are finding veterans and spouses who would benefit from the assistance and to provide it as they were in the hunt for employment. The right place means we are helping veterans and their families in our community. The right reasons are simply that. People and organizations who are looking to engage to help veterans not for personal profit, wealth, prestige, or power.

Our ACP events ended up being very popular because they gave veterans the opportunity to come into Fortune 500 companies and network with employees and experience corporate culture firsthand. UPS, GE, and AT&T would take turns hosting the ACP events, but UPS always had the largest crowd of participants, volunteers, and the best speakers, which was a feat because the UPS VBRG was not funded. The other ACP partner companies would put on a nice spread of food and beverages, but I served water, cookies, and popcorn with an occasional pizza I funded out of my own pocket.

All our ACP events had a panel discussion which provided expertise from veterans who had made the transition and included hiring managers and executives. We had networking prior to the panel discussions which provided a solid opportunity to connect to our companies, nonprofits, and each other and provided opportunities for mock job interviews and resume reviews. We supported ACP quarterly events for three years and these experiences would be a big part on my journey to VETLANTA.

Jordan Kellett and I hosting an American Corporate Partners event at UPS in 2014

9
JOURNEY INTO VETLANTA

*While we can never do enough to show grat-
itude to our nation's defenders, we can always
do a little more.* –Gary Sinise, Actor, Humanitarian,
and Musician

I received a phone call in December 2013 that would change
my life. David, Wattenmaker was a recently separated Marine
Corps officer who had started a yearlong leadership program
with Coca-Cola and during one of his rotations, he was assigned
to work for John Phillips. John is a retired Army Lieutenant
Colonel who served half of his Army career in artillery and the
other half in finance. John is enthusiastic about supporting veterans and has written a military transition book called *Boots to
Loafers, Finding Your New True North.* More importantly, John
had overseen the Coca-Cola Veterans Day program for many
years which is a very big deal for a company that is steeped
in its history of supporting veterans. John has done amazing
things for veterans for a very long time. He is currently one
of the civilian aids to the Secretary of the Army for Georgia
and has been inducted to the Georgia Military Veterans Hall
of Fame, and he is now one of my best friends. We occasionally poke each other in the eye, but we've always resolved our
issues and partnered well during our VETLANTA journeys.

The three founders of VETLANTA, John Phillips, Lloyd Knight, David Wattenmaker

During this period, many of the Fortune 500 Companies across the country had stood up or were getting ready to stand up VBRG/Veteran Affinity Groups/Veteran Networks. John believed this would be a good opportunity to get all the leaders of these groups in the Atlanta area together in a room to talk about what each company was doing to support veterans. He later admitted that he was under the assumption that Coca-Cola was the only company in Atlanta that was doing anything significant for veterans. John tasked David with contacting all the companies and extending the invite to the first meeting.

A month later, about two dozen veteran leaders from about fifteen companies met at Coca-Cola's Windy Hill Campus in

North Atlanta. This was the Who's Who in Atlanta including UPS, AT&T, GE, Home Depot, Coca-Cola, Delta Airlines, Georgia Tech, McKesson, and Georgia Pacific. Jordan and I attended the meeting together and it might surprise some of you who know me that I didn't say a total of ten words that night. I was completely blown away with the experience and personalities in the room, which included executives, several attendees with doctorates, several who had written books, and everyone had been in the veteran support space a whole lot longer than me. Jordan was equally intimidated but also impressed with the spread of food as Coca-Cola really was able to throw a party. That night, Jordan smuggled a sandwich in his pocket which is something we still laugh at today.

What we discovered at this meeting was astonishing. Our companies were doing huge things to support veterans nationally, and more important, locally. Collectively, and I don't exaggerate these numbers, our companies were hiring tens of thousands of veterans each year, our company foundations were donating tens of millions of dollars to veteran causes, and our employees were volunteering tens of thousands of hours each year with veteran nonprofits. What we also figured out was none of the VBRGs in Atlanta were talking to each other. We had the potential of building an amazing network, however a network is not a network if it's not connected. That meeting was so good, we decided to have a second meeting several weeks later and that meeting was another important step in the journey to VETLANTA.

The second meeting was focused on the good, the bad, and the ugly of the veteran's space. The good, the bad, and the ugly can be found in employers, government agencies, businesses, academia, healthcare, nonprofit organizations, and individual contributors. The good is someone or an organization that is providing the right assistance at the right time for the right people at the right location and for the right reasons. The bad is twofold. The first is an organization that provides valuable services in the space but is overly focused on fund raising or glory versus providing service deliverables. The example that comes to mind is Wounded Warrior Project (WWP) under their former leadership.

While I been figuratively punched in face for saying this in the past, WWP was too focused on selling merchandise, celebrity engagement, fundraising, and the wasteful spending, all of which has been well documented in the media. According to a CBS New report, "Americans donate hundreds of millions of dollars each year to the charity, expecting their money will help some of the 52,000 wounded in Iraq and Afghanistan. But CBS News found Wounded Warrior Project spends 40 to 50 percent on overhead, including extravagant parties. Other veteran charities have overhead costs of 10 to 15 percent." There are multiple other large veteran service organizations that fit the same bill and we really can't provide too much assistance to organizations that fit the bad criteria because they simply don't listen. John Phillips and I on several occasions were abused on social media by WWP employees at the start of VETLANTA as they felt threatened by us especially by our desire to highlight their competitors.

In defense of WWP, they did fire their CEO and COO in March 2016 and named retired US Army Lieutenant General Michael Linnington as their new CEO several months later. General Linnington has done a solid job transforming the organization and, while we have not been able to form a solid strategic partnership, they are in better shape today. Several weeks after General Linnington took the CEO job, he came down to Atlanta for America's Warrior Partnership's annual Warrior Community Integration Symposium where I was moderating the opening event. Upon arriving at the venue, I was asked by the host if I wanted to meet the general, which I flatly refused. She asked me why and I very brashly told her that I'd made a promise to myself that if I ever met WWP leadership, I would tell them exactly what I felt about their organization. The host came back five minutes later and said that the general wanted to meet me and wanted to hear all my grievances.

Wow, did I step in it. I took a big gulp and walked over to him. The general is in amazing shape and a bit taller than me, and he is knowingly or unknowingly an expert at the Johnson Treatment. The Johnson Treatment is a strategy used by President Lyndon B. Johnson where he would stand very close to someone and lean in to invade personnel space and start talking. I was a bit intimidated but laid out all my complaints and observations without hesitation. The general, to his credit, listened politely and responded graciously and professionally. He thanked me for my candor and for having the guts to speak with him and he said that he was just in his second week and would call me the next week to follow up. On Monday morning I received his call, and he once again thanked me, provided details on the changes he was making, and we agreed to have his COO speak at the next VETLANTA Summit, which he courageously did.

The next subcategory in bad are those organizations and individuals who have solid intent, and their hearts and souls are in the right place, however they just don't have the business sense or leadership ability to ever be effective or efficient with your donor dollars or volunteer hours. We try to help these organizations but there are just so many nonprofits that are started unnecessarily and without solid leadership or solid business and operating plans and many flounder in infectiveness and go under.

The ugly are the fraudsters, scammers, and schemers out there and unfortunately, they are prevalent. Even worse, many of them are fellow veterans. They are visible in the community and events and are very bold in their mission to separate us and our organizations from our money and assets. I don't know how many times I've been called with the same spiel, which goes something like this: "I have this incredible business opportunity and we are going to make at least two dozen veterans rich, and I could approach anyone with this opportunity but I'm selecting the veteran community because of my love of veterans and my generosity." These fraudsters are so prevalent in the community that I could fill up a series of books on examples but I'm going to only share several of the more shocking ones.

One of my friends works in the office of a congressman in this area and he was approached by a person trying to start a veterans-in-farming nonprofit. They explained that veterans would work the fields on this farm and in return they would get free or discounted rent and would gain farming experience. When my friend asked how much the veterans would get paid for the work the guy acted insulted and said they wouldn't be paid anything. If this scheme sounds familiar it's sharecropping, which was largely eliminated in the United States in the early 1950s.

One of the first fraudulent groups I encountered was early in our history when I was vetting organizations to decide who to put on the stage at a summit. I was approached by these two veterans who claimed their PTSD was largely cured during a cruise the two of them took together earlier in the year and they were starting a veteran cruises nonprofit. I asked them a series of questions like what would the formal program be, would there be any counselors on the ship, what medical pre-screening would be done, what were the post-cruise plans? They said the responsibility of their nonprofit was only the cruise and the funds would be used to pay for their cruise tickets and expenses, and they would be on the cruise to mentor veterans who self-identified with PTSD. It was funny and shocking at the same time, and they disappeared from our radar shortly afterward.

Sometimes, good people and organizations lose their way and move from the good over to the bad and ugly categories. We had a very reputable nonprofit that had done really good work in the nonprofit arena for several decades and had formed amazing relationships with multiple Fortune 500 companies. Unfortunately, they decided to chase the money and were adding anything that stuck which had the possibility of bringing in funds for the organization. During a breakfast meeting with the CEO and his spouse, I asked a question that I always ask organizations that are looking to partner with VETLANTA and that is "What specifically are you doing to support veterans and their families?" The first three attempts to answer came out as a word salad that would make Vice President Kamala Harris cringe. On the third answer, his wife just blurted out that when they go on trips, she saves the soap and shampoo from the hotel and donates it to the local veteran's homeless shelter. It was a shocking surprise and very sad to see someone with such great connections and a solid track record of providing community service shame themselves in doing something like this especially at the expense of our military veterans.

We would see another case of ugly at one of our early employment events which happened to be at the UPS Global Headquarters in Atlanta. One of the keynote speakers was an Army veteran who was in the Georgia House and one of top three gubernatorial candidates. He was set to spend an hour with the crowd during networking prior to taking the stage. He ended up missing the entire networking hour and we had to start the speaking session late because we could not find him. I checked with security and confirmed that he had entered the building but had disappeared. It turns out, a veteran non-profit in attendance was supposed to have a meeting with him earlier in the day but he cancelled and told them he would talk to them at the VETLANTA event that evening.

When the folks from this nonprofit arrived, they told UPS security that they needed a conference room and had cleared it with me, which was a lie. When our VIP showed up, they whisked him into the conference room and told him they cleared the meeting with me, which was another lie. They held him in that room until I figured out what had happened and came to get him and put him on stage. I was furious but kept it together and remained professional. The next day, the head jack wagon of this group called me and tried to place nice. I reviewed their behavior from the previous evening and told them a lack of integrity was not in the best interests of veterans and their families and let him know they were officially blocked from future VETLANTA events. This guy had the nerve to then call our VBRG Executive Advisor to explain that this whole thing was a communication misunderstanding which, was lie number three. The Air Force has three core values and number one is integrity first. Without integrity, all else is lost.

At the end of the second meeting, after we had spent three hours talking about the good, the bad, and the ugly, I made the statement that we needed to connect the network so we could advertise the good, try to help the bad, and isolate the ugly. We were all motivated and encouraged and decided to start weekly phone meetings to take advantage of the momentum we'd established during the first two meetings. Fortunately, or unfortunately, it was decided on the next call that we should solely focus on having veteran employment fairs.

It was unfortunate because this was a bad idea for many reasons. First, there were already several nonprofits and for-profit organizations that were hosting regularly scheduled job fairs and most of our companies were committed to supporting those. Second, we didn't have anyone one in our ranks who worked in human resources, nor did we have any way to effectively recruit candidates outside of word of mouth. This really ended up killing our momentum as the number of participants on the call dropped from forty+ to just myself, David Wattenmaker, and a third member from SunTrust who dropped out later. John was no longer able to spend quality time effectively leading our efforts as he had new work commitments that severely limited his engagement.

I had been mostly quiet and largely deferred to others in the group to lead, but since I saw the huge potential with this group, I attended every meeting. After one meeting, David called me up and provided pertinent direction, "Lloyd, you are a great leader and as resolute and enthusiastic as everyone else who has been involved to this point, why don't you pick up the ball and run with it to see if you are able to regain the momentum and get better results." I thought about it and quickly jumped at the opportunity.

If you've been to a VETLANTA Summit, you've probably heard me joke about all the breakfast meetings I've attended over the years and that I weighed 150 pounds before VETLANTA and 260 now. While both of those numbers are exaggerated, this is where the breakfast meetings started. I began to have meetings with anyone who had an opinion on what we should do with the forum we'd established. I met with lawyers, fellow UPSers, VBRG leaders, consultants, veterans, and business leaders, and while I didn't know it at the time since I was so far out of my element, these were our stakeholders. Two of the most important at the time were lawyers. The first lawyer, Scott Bass, was not a veteran. Scott is now a board member, and I was skeptical at first as I tried to find out if he was the good, the bad, or the ugly. Scott is an amazing supporter, friend, and family man, and I value his perspective. The second was Kevin Horgan. Kevin is also a board member and is now a retired

UPSer. He is a Marine Corps veteran and father and father-in-law to two Navy veterans.

I first met Kevin at an American Corporate Partners event I was hosting at my building. He walked into the room and started giving a Marine veteran in the room a hard time for not wearing his Marine Corps lapel pin. I introduced myself and Kevin in his normal gruffness made fun that I was an Air Force veteran, so he didn't immediately impress me. My first thought was *Just what I need, a Marine in my life.* Kevin was exactly what I needed. He always tells you his opinion and, while we don't always agree, most of his ideas are solid; and when we don't, he salutes and carries on. By the way, at the ACP event, he took off his lapel pin and gave it to that young Marine. I never had much need for Marines when I was in the Air Force, but for VETLANA I've surrounded myself with Marines because they make it happen. Semper Fi!

Kevin Horgan and I volunteering at a homeless Point in Time Count in Atlanta in 2016

I had six breakfast meetings over the next couple of weeks at 6:30 AM and collected data, information, and opinions from over several dozen people. I routinely talked with Kevin and Scott and made decisions which the two of them would use to create a charter to guide our actions and strategy going forward. I had no idea that those early decisions we made would differentiate us from anything else out there, be a catalyst for continued growth, and take us from a handful of veterans sitting around the table to an organization of thousands of members with a respected brand.

The first big decision was to organize ourselves as a chartered club and not as a non-profit or an LLC. I didn't believe people would trust us if we went the LLC route as it could very easily be self-serving and seen as a profit driver. A 501C organization seemed the better choice, but that would require administrative oversight and funding and I wanted to form an organization that could be agile, flexible, lean, and not constrained by red tape and bureaucracy. I was sure we could get funding from one of the Fortune 500 companies, however we didn't want our companies to shift funds to us and potentially be taking funding away from an existing nonprofit that was providing value to the veteran community. Fortune 500 companies are very generous in their giving but there are millions of requests per year and there are simply not enough funds to meet even a fraction of the requests.

The next decision was to charter our club not to accept or give any monetary funds. We wanted our focus to be on volunteerism and collaboration and not be clouded by raising money or deciding how, where, and when to distribute funds. We assumed we really wouldn't need funding and any expense that did come up we would be able to handle it by passing the hat around the board and through in-kind support. I never thought in a million years that we would grow to where we are today. John Phillips and I often joke around and say if we were smart enough to develop a ten-year plan when we started, we would have thought too small as we never recognized the full potential of what we'd started.

The next decision was to open our club to anyone who wanted to help veterans and their families and not just the Fortune 500 veteran groups. We opened the club to individual contributors, nonprofit organizations, businesses of all sizes, academia, and government organizations. Our next action was one of the hardest and most frustrating things I've ever had to do and that was to pick a name and design a logo. Thank goodness we had some amazing help as our first real in-kind investor stepped up to help. Marshall Lauck, Marine Corps veteran, and former COO of J. Walter Thompson Atlanta offered his service.

J. Walter Thompson (JWT) was an advertisement holding company incorporated in 1896 by American advertising pioneer James Walter Thompson. Mr. Thompson was a Commodore in the Navy from 1864 to 1866 and served in the Marine Corps from 1867-1868. The company, after an acquisition and merger, is now known as Wunderman Thompson. They have been the US Marine Corps lead advertising agency for an astounding seventy-five years and are the creators of those brilliant recruiting commercials which have outshined all the other branches of service for a very long time. What's even more astounding is they didn't charge the government for their services for several decades.

Marshall at once appreciated what we were trying to do and assigned several volunteer resources from JWT to help. At first, I did second-guess who he'd picked because he'd assigned junior people who were not attached to the Marine Corps advertising account or military veterans. This ended up being brilliant as they didn't have any preconceived notions and the consulting assistance they provided was exceptional.

After they helped us formulate what we were trying to carry out, we went about finding a name.

This proved to be super challenging, and we had so many varying opinions on names including whether we should use an acronym, if the name should have our mission, or if it should be a military term. We narrowed it down to five names and decided to conduct a vote at a meeting at JWT's headquarters in Atlanta. We did a live vote with those present and chose the name North Georgia Military Business Resource Council. This name had won the vote, but no one in the room was overly thrilled with it. About ten seconds after the vote, Jordan Kellett out of nowhere just blurted out "That name sucks; what about VETLANTA?" The buzz in the room hit the rafters and we at once voted again and unanimously chose VETLANTA. Several years later, the producers of *Animal Planet* contacted Scott Bass to enquire about the name as they were getting ready to start a new veterinarian show in Atlanta and wanted to use our name. Scott very quickly applied to have the name trademarked and we passed the hat amongst the board to pay for it. Jordan and his wife would go on to have two children over the next several years and he was promoted several times to manager and didn't have the time to be able to be very involved with VETLANTA. He's since left UPS and moved back home to Charleston, South Carolina. He's landed a great job and no longer must smuggle sandwiches from events though a part of me believes he still does.

JWT provided amazing help with the logo. They consulted with us for several hours and a week later came back with seven designs to vote on. One looked like the old OJ Simpson television commercial where he was running through the airport with a briefcase. Some members had an issue with the logo we ended up choosing as it resembled President Obama's campaign logo and we were striving to be apolitical. One of the account executives from JWT supplied wisdom and said "If we do this right, people will be talking about VETLANTA long after President Obama's second term'" which turned out to be true and spot-on advice. Our next task was to formulate a strategy and brand.

Most of our first members came from the Fortune 500 companies so we decided to implement a brand strategy like how our companies operated. We wanted our brand to be something the community trusted and was well respected. We decided to protect the brand image by vetting all organizations we partnered with, policing each other's social media across the board, having strict standards for anyone we gave stage time to, and not letting anyone make money directly off our efforts. We've had many individuals and businesses that have tried to make money by aligning with us, which has become frustrating at times. While many are credible, some also fall into the "ugly" category.

If we'd let every wealth manager and home loan company on the stage that has approached us over the years, our summits would be a 24/7 sales pitch, and I'm not exaggerating as it's been in the thousands. Many make the approach as "I'm not here to sell anything, I just want to help veterans, and I can provide training to your members." On several occasions, we've accepted their offers to provide training but, after we scrubbed their training materials of any direct sales info, they quickly disappeared. Normally when approached, we invite these folks to our summits and explain their opportunity to engage will be during the networking. Many don't bother attending but a few have become routine attendees and are now providing real and credible value to our members.

Another thing we did to protect our brand image was to stay out of the political fray by being apolitical. This has been tough as many of the board members have big opinions on politics and candidates, but we collectively decided and have continually reinforced over the years that jumping into any political fight would turn off many of our members and just wasn't the right thing to do in support of our mission, which was to support veterans. We do occasionally have state, local, and federal elected officials attend and even speak at our summits, but we always reinforce there is no campaigning allowed and their focus needs to be how they support the military, veterans, and their families.

Several years later, our apolitical strategy would be seriously tested for the first time in the days after Donald Trump won the election in 2016. We had recently partnered with the Sierra Club to do a veteran's camping trip in the North Georgia Mountains, and we had over two dozen members sign up. There was a real buzz that we were onto something special, and this would be another opportunity for VETLANTA to connect veterans and a great conduit between our summits and a win for the Sierra Club as they were looking to get more involved in the veteran space. Within days of the election, the point of contact from the Sierra Club started emailing disparaging things about the election and the president elect to all the veterans who had signed up for the trip.

When we reminded him that we are an apolitical organization and, as far as VETLANTA was concerned, we wouldn't take a side either way. We reinforced our commitment to partner on the trip but mandated that the political emails stop. What we got in response was shocking as we were dressed down in a mean-spirited and unprofessional way. John and I consulted with each other and cancelled the trip. It was very disappointing and a sign of the hysteria that has become so prevalent in our country today. It was also a solid test of our strategy which we passed with flying colors and highlighted that we could indeed be effective without taking a political stance. It's been disappointing to see several Atlanta-based companies who we based our brand strategy on needlessly go political over the last several years on issues that seriously alienated many of their loyal customers.

VETLANTA over the years has become known for our quarterly summits. In the beginning we gave stage time to any organization which was supporting veterans and their families who wanted to get the word out. The network was largely unconnected and not many of us were fully aware of all the organizations out there and what their mission were, so we provided our summits as the avenue for these organizations to advertise and for us to get educated. Our early summits were three hours straight of PowerPoint and it was not unusual for us to put twenty-five+ groups on stage and have over 300 slides. While it was painful, we also ran these events with expert efficiency, and I enforced a strict deadline of seven minutes for all organizations and would pull speakers off the stage if they went over.

These events always finished on-time and we came to be known for hosting well-orchestrated events with precision. We also looked to constantly improve our summits and would have after-action meetings after each summit that could be brutal at times. At UPS, we had a culture called constructive dissatisfaction and used this approach for these meetings. There were often hurt feelings but in these early days, we always made it a habit to leave the meeting on friendly terms and go break bread with each other. These poke-you-in- the-eye after-action meetings controlled our egos and made our events even better.

In those first two years, I practically did all the required coordination including finding a host, setting the agenda, creating and sending the invites, vetting, and prepping the speakers, setting up the room, consolidating the slides, and managing event day. I always opened our summits with presidents' comments and often I was just completely exhausted when I came off the stage. A couple of days after one summit, Kevin Horgan invited me to lunch and gave me some straightforward advice that really changed how we operated going forward. He told me that I needed to be the face of VETLANTA and should be kissing babies and shaking hands and not burdened with the tactical level details of the summits and we had volunteers who would passionately help. I believe Kevin was surprised when I named him the Chief Operations Officer during the next board meeting and he and the entire board have done a fantastic job over the years in letting me be front and center while they've handled the logistics and operations.

Our summits are supported by hosts who provide in-kind support including providing a venue, food and beverages, and nametags. Special thanks to Coca-Cola for providing non-alcoholic beverages at our summits for the last nine years. In the early days, all our summits were held at corporate offices; however we quickly outgrew most corporate space options and are blessed to have supporters who rent venues across Metro Atlanta for our events including Mercedes Benz Stadium, Twelve Hotel Ball Room, the College Football Hall of Fame, and the Clay National Guard Center to name a few. We've had many amazing hosts over the years including UPS, KPMG, Coca-Cola, GE, Kimberly Clark, JWT, McKesson, Turner, Southern Company, Deloitte, the Knights of Columbus, Morgan Stanley, Georgia Tech, the Arthur Blank Family of Businesses, the Georgia National Guard, FISERV, JP Morgan Chase, Rheem, Kaiser Permanente, the College Football Hall of Fame, and The Warrior Alliance. These hosts sponsor our events and help VETLANTA perform our mission.

Over the years we've had some incredible speakers including Governor Brian Kemp, USMC veteran and retired UFC fighter Brian Stann, Sergeant Major of the Army Ray Chandler, Acting

Secretary of the Army Patrick Murphy, Colonel Tom Manion, Amy Looney Heffernan, Medal of Honor Recipient Hershel "Woody" Williams, Medal of Honor Recipient David Bellavia, Medal of Honor Recipient Florent Groberg, Vietnam POW survivor Colonel Dewey Waddell, Senator Raphael Warnock, and Congressman Andrew Clyde to name a few.

Kicking of a summit at UPS with, left to right, Navy SEAL Jared Ogden, Acting Secretary of the Army Patrick Murphy, Colonel (Retired) Dewey Wayne Waddel

I have fond memories of several speakers. Sergeant Major of the Army Ray Chandler was one of our first keynote speakers and was spending time in Atlanta when he was deciding what city to move to when he retired from the Army. He called me as I was headed home from work and had stopped to get gas. I answered the phone to hear "Hi, Lloyd, this Ray." I ran through the rolodex in my brain and replied, "I don't know anyone named

Ray." He explained who he was and agreed to be our first well-known keynote speaker. We had Woody Williams on our first COVID Virtual Summit and when I introduced him, I mentioned the Navy named a ship after him and he told me "First Sergeant, I may be ninety-eight years old, but I'm still alive, so the Navy named the ship *for* me not *after* me." We had planned on getting Woody to an in-person summit last year, but he has since passed away. Semper Fi, Marine.

Amy Looney Heffernan and Colonel Tom Manion were huge for both Suzan and I to have as keynote speakers. Suzan had read the book *Brothers Forever,* which recounts the personal story of how two Naval academy roommates—Colonel Manon's son, US Marine Travis Manion, and Amy's husband, US Navy SEAL Brendan Looney—defined a generation's sacrifice after 9/11, and how their loved ones carry on. This book was written by Colonel Manion and Tom Sileo, and we hand the chance to meet Tom Sileo at a book signing in Marietta which he attended with Brian Stann. Brian was running Hire Heroes USA at the time and a VETLANTA supporter and he'd been friends with Travis and Brendan at the Naval Academy. Both signed Suzan's book and spent time with her talking about these amazing men and their story.

The next year, I had the opportunity to hear Colonel Manion speak at an event hosted by JWT and was so moved that I took five pages of notes and came up with several new ideas on how VETLANTA could make more of an impact in our community. The next year he spoke at a VETLANTA summit hosted by Coca-Cola and was a huge hit with our members. I had been introduced to Amy and she was a keynote speaker at a VETLANTA virtual summit and did such a fine job telling her story as everyone on was moved by her resilience. A couple of years before Suzan passed away, I had the opportunity to attend a veterans' event at the White House and was blessed to be invited by Marshall Lauck to a Bob Woodruff event, which was attended by Chairman of the Joint Chiefs of Staff, General Joseph Dunford and his predecessor, General Martin Dempsey. While we met both and got our pictures taken, the real highlight for Suzan was Amy was also in attendance. She was very friendly and sat with us, spending over an hour talking with Suzan.

Suzan with Colonel (ret.) Tom Manion during a VETLANTA Summit at Coca-Cola in 2017

Suzan with Chairman of the Joint Chiefs of Staff, General Joseph Dunford, in Washington, DC, in 2019

The Travis Manion Foundation (TMF) is a 501(c)3 non-profit organization that unites communities to strengthen America's national character by empowering veterans and families of fallen heroes to develop and lead future generations. In 2007, First Lt Travis Manion (USMC) was killed in Iraq while saving his wounded teammates. Today, Travis's legacy lives on in the words he spoke before leaving for his final deployment, "If not me, then who ..."

Guided by this mantra, veterans continue their service, develop strong relationships with their communities, and thrive in their post-military lives by serving as character role models to youth. As a result, communities prosper and the character of our nation's heroes lives on in the next generation.

Amy is the vice president of the organization, and Travis's sister, Ryan Manion, is the president. They have a chapter in Atlanta that is run by Jason Dodge, one of our long-time members, and Suzan and I were able to volunteer many times at local Travis Manion Foundation events. Suzan and I also had the opportunity to visit the graves of the two "brothers" at Arlington during a trip. We were both moved to tears which was a first during my many trips to Arlington over the years. When Suzan passed away, I'd requested, in lieu flowers, contributions be made to the Travis Manion Foundation in her name.

David Bellavia was also a big highlight for the two us, our board, and our members. He was very gracious with his time agreeing to speak at the summit, participate in a boss lift Blackhawk ride, speak at one of our companies, attend a dinner with the board, and come on "Supply Chain Now Radio, Veteran Voices," which was a podcast I had started with my good friend, Air Force veteran Scott Luton. David travels with his actual Medal of Honor, which is dirty because he constantly takes it off and hands it to people to hold. Keep your eye out for David as he's going to do even bigger things in the future.

Scott Luton, Medal of Honor Recipient David Bellavia, and Lloyd after a "Supply Chain Now" radio show in 2019

In addition to these well-known veterans, we've had some amazing local speakers that have blown the doors off our summits over the years with one of my favorites being Mike Reynolds, a long time VETLANTA member and recent keynote speaker. If you've met Mike, you know he is hero with amazing determination, resolve, and drive and an incredible sense of humor with a quick wit. Mike's also one of the smartest soldiers I've ever met, which is something that I'm disappointed took me so long to figure out.

He is a retired US Army Master Sergeant and Georgia native. While he was still in high school, Mike began a career with the fire department and emergency medical services.

After college, he joined the US Army as a flight medic and traveled the globe. He spent almost four years as the flight medic at Dobbins Air Reserve Base in Marietta, Georgia, and deployed to Northern Iraq to head a military ambulance service. After sustaining a significant traumatic brain injury, he returned to the U.S. for treatment where he was judged "Unfit for Duty" just before he began his eighteenth year of military service and was forced to retire. Mike's recovery has been slow but steady as he's endured multiple hospitalizations and years of cognitive, speech, vocational, physical, and rehabilitation therapy, but even with all of this Mike has started his next career in farming and his desire to support fellow veterans and their families has never wavered.

Together with his wife Kim and their two children, they share the joy and commitment of living a farming lifestyle. Recognizing the importance of healthier living, the Reynolds have dedicated their farm to providing a healthier alternative through providing a cleaner beef. He is also the self-designated Chief Farming Officer for HERO Agriculture, which helps veterans with reintegration into civilian life and adjustment to a "New Normal." Through the development of a comprehensive agricultural plan, individuals gain the education and networking skills required to create their own agricultural operation. With the help and support of HERO Agriculture, veterans learn the skills to create their agricultural business.

Visiting Mike Reynolds at his farm in 2022

Tyler Bowser is another good friend who was a memorable summit speaker. Tyler is featured in my UPS Jim Casey Community Service Award video. which can be found at https://www.youtube.com/watch?v=pbQCzWajYns. Tyler was a homeless veteran being housed at a local veterans shelter in Atlanta called the Veterans Empowerment Organization. Tyler is an Air Force veteran and, through a series of bad luck, bad choices, and health issues, he found himself living in his car. Tyler's testimonial was powerful, and it's been a privilege to watch him heal, grow, aspire, and succeed.

We've had several more warriors like Mike and Tyler who have taken the stage and told their gut-wrenching stories not to draw attention to themselves but to draw attention to a cause which is always to support veterans and their families. These testimonials highlight that results are more than just data in a spreadsheet. Success at times is measured one veteran at a time and we need to ensure we focus on the people and not just the data.

Another person I want to highlight who has taken the stage many times at our summits is VETLANTA Board Member, Amy Stevens. Amy will probably hate that I'm spending several paragraphs on her as she never seeks attention, awards, or prestige. Amy is a Navy veteran serving from 1974-1995 and is now a licensed counselor, helping others like her connect with resources or people who can support them mentally and emotionally through this Facebook group "Georgia Military Women," which has several thousand members and has banded together not only to help each other but to advocate for female veteran issues across Georgia and the country.

I met Amy very early on in the VETLANTA journey and we butted heads almost immediately. I thought *Who is this 5 foot 1, doctor and why does she keep poking me in the eye?* Over the next couple of years, our attitudes aligned closer to each other as we've become more seasoned in the veteran support space Amy is someone I trust and I'm thankful for her friendship and support when Suzan became very ill in 2020 and during my journey after she passed away in 2022. Recently I went on a VETLANTA hike and one of our female members pulled up in a car which had license plates with "Woman Veteran" on it. I asked her about it, and she was so thrilled with the tags as people have stopped asking her about her husband's military service. I'm assuming that Amy and Georgia Military Women had something to do with these new tags. Ladies, thank you for your service in and out of uniform and keep up the fight.

10
THE VETLANTA
JOURNEY CONTINUES

My fellow Americans: ask not what your country can do for you—ask what you can do for your country. —President John F. Kennedy

When we opened our summits to anyone who wanted to attend who has a desire to support veterans and their families, we saw immediate growth especially with the non-profits. They saw the likes of UPS, Delta, AT&T, GE, Coca-Cola, Home Depot, Georgia Power, Georgia Pacific, McKesson, and others involved and they showed up and many believed there would be instant financial benefit, but they were very wrong. As John Phillips constantly says, "VETLANTA is networking on steroids" and while we connect the dots, we don't control any purse strings. In fact, at UPS I've never directly applied for a grant with the UPS Foundation. I take great pride that the foundation calls on me as a trusted advisor, so I never want money to cloud my judgement or create the appearance that it has.

Some of these nonprofits showed up and left after not securing an early promise of financial gain. The ones who got our concept stayed and benefited. If you've never tried to request a grant from a corporate foundation, it can be challenging and near impossible. There are only enough funds to meet a handful of the requests so it can be a challenge finding the grant process and it's even harder to find someone at a foundation to talk to. The magic solution is to find an employee from within a company who will advocate for your nonprofit. Another hint is to start with volunteer opportunities and *do not* start off the relationship with a fund request.

I always compare this process to dating. As the VBRG Chair at UPS, I was in high demand with the veteran non-profits. It always amazed me that many times during the first meeting, these groups would ask for money and most of the time it was eight and even nine figures. They were wanting to go all the way with me without courting me or my company first. According to the MyRelationshipCenter.com, the goal of dating is to get to know each other, have fun together, discover similarities, and learn about life expectations, goals, and dreams. This is all true when seeking a corporate champion and donor dollars from the large company foundations.

There is one group that really figured this out very early on and that was Soldiers Angels in Atlanta. This group's Georgia rep was Dianne Moore and she and her husband Steve are as enthusiastic about serving veterans as anyone I know. When we opened the summits to nonprofits, they showed up and you couldn't miss them. At the time, most of our attendees would wear formal business attire and they showed up wearing jeans and polos and both have wild hair, so they stood out big time. We are about the same age, so I really appreciate they are musicians and create these super 1980s style music videos. You can check out their videos on YouTube by searching for The Cranberry Merchants.

While I might have been underwhelmed at first with their appearance, they impressed me during our very first conversation as I saw they had the passion, determination, smarts, and business sense to be effective. Dianne and Steve started showing up for everything and started to build trust as we saw results. They transitioned from just being an attendee, to getting a table during networking, to even getting stage time at several summits. With this trust, they found company advocates and volunteers from a handful of the Fortune 500 companies including UPS. After a year of showing up, being visible, and focusing on recruiting volunteers, multiple small grants followed, and they became my poster child nonprofit when introducing new organizations to VETLANTA. Unfortunately, the Moores are no longer part of Soldiers Angels, but they still do come to an occasional summit.

We have been blessed to find some solid advocates who have helped us to continue to find our way and spearheaded continuous improvement and we've continued to evolve. Our first executive advisors included Steve Cannon from the Arthur Blank Family Company of Businesses, John Tien a former Managing Director at Citi, and Chris Peck, my mentor at UPS and now a retired VP. John has since joined the Biden administration and is no longer directly involved. Several wonderful consultants have jumped in and provided in-kind support including McKinsey and Company, Slalom Consulting, JWT Atlanta, and Deloitte. Through these consulting efforts we developed a formal mission statement and have added to it over the years. Our mission is to make the greater Atlanta area the premier community in the country for veterans and their families to work, live, play, and pray.

We added Zack Knight to the board, and he's helped us transform. Zack is an Army veteran and one of the folks who inspired me to write this book. He was also there for me after Suzan passed away and for that I'll always be grateful. It's not unusual for people to call Zack my son but we are not related. One of our goals over the years is to have events which connect veterans between the summits, but we had not had a lot of success prior to Zack jumping in. We've partnered with Zack's company to host monthly BATL Brew sessions which are monthly meetups at a local brewery which connect the business and veteran community. VETLANTA Views is one of my favorite things we've ever done and it's networking with a physical fitness component. We either hike or do a guided workout and I believe this program will grow significantly in the future as the world starts to normalize after COVID. The third connecting event and the reason we've added *pray* to our mission is I've been inspired to connect veteran believers using the VETLANTA model and we've recently started Veterans in Faith, which will eventually turn into monthly meetups.

Through the consulting we received, we've continually explored if we should change our strategy and become a 501C nonprofit organization. Each time, we've decided to remain a chartered club. While this continues to restrict direct funding it allows us to be flexible and agile, simplifies engagement with the Fortune 500 companies, allows us to add government employees to our board, and allows us to not be influenced by money which allows us to openly discuss the good, the bad, and the ugly in the space. We've continued to grow over the years, and we currently have over 7,000 members registered on our website and, prior to COVID, we averaged 550 attendees per quarterly summit.

While growth is important, it's not as important as ensuring we get the right people in the right room for the right reasons at the right time, and size doesn't guarantee quality. One thing I'm proud of is our focus on the greater Atlanta area, which is our community. Over the years, we've had this big call to nationalize, become a nonprofit, and add salaried positions to the organization. This would really change the strategy and our intent to be focused on our local community, so we've resisted.

We have supplied our charter, lessons learned, and best practices to over three dozen cities across the country. Several groups have tried to start something similar in their communities, but none has been as successful for several reasons. Some have aligned their efforts with local governments and have been bogged down by red tape and politics. Others have decided to become a nonprofit and, with our model, it just has not worked as it's very hard to go from the outside to the inside of the Fortune 500s.

I'm also proud that through our efforts to highlight Atlanta as a veteran destination several new veteran nonprofits have been successfully created in our area including The Warrior Alliance and multiple nonprofits have opened branches in Atlanta including FourBlock, the US Chamber of Commerce Hiring our Heroes Corporate Fellowship, the Travis Manion Foundation, Team RWB, and Bunker Labs. We love that nonprofit organizations see VETLANTA as a partner and enabler as some in the beginning saw us as competition and a threat. There aren't enough donor dollars to go around, so the space is highly competitive and we were seen as competition at the beginning as we were getting a lot of attention and a lot of support. Several groups have tried to create VETLANTA type of organizations in the greater Atlanta area but they have focused on fundraising in the beginning and none have been all that effective. My marching orders to the board from the beginning is we should not see anyone as competition since we don't need funds and we welcome any organization that supports veterans and their families.

We've been successful over the years attracting new companies to join VETLANTA and part of this success has been due to my elevator speech, and I want to share my opening.

"Good afternoon, my name is Lloyd Knight. I'm a retired Air Force veteran, Co-Founder and President of VETLANTA. We are a chartered club looking to make Atlanta the premier community in the country for veterans and their families to work, live, play, and pray. As I tell you about VETLANTA, the first thing I must first tell you is we don't want your money." When I mention that we don't want any money, most people really start paying attention. Leaders in companies and foundations almost become tone deaf because of the sheer number of requests we get for donations, so its well-received when I explain that our focus is on collaboration, volunteerism, and networking.

One of our more interesting engagements was with Bob McDonald, the eigth United States Secretary of Veteran Affairs. I had met Bob shortly after he landed the role and visited UPS corporate headquarters to meet with our senior leadership. I call him Bob as he will let you know when you meet him to use his first name and not his title or any formal salutation. Bob is an Army veteran and is the retired Chairman, President, and CEO of Procter & Gamble. Bob had been briefed on VETLANTA and we received a call that said he would once again be traveling to Atlanta and wanted to meet. Me, John, and Matt Grob, one of our former board members, showed up at the VA Hospital thinking it would be a large contingent of veteran groups in the meeting and it ended up just being us with Bob. He was intrigued by how we'd been able to build VETLATNA from scratch without any funding and hold these amazing sum-mits. Over the next ninety minutes, we went over our history, discussed best practices, lessons learned, and supplied some feedback on the Community Veteran Engagement Board.

[INSERT PICTURE #3. CAPTION: Left to Right: Lloyd, Secretary of Veterans Affairs Bob McDonald, Matt Grob, and John Phillips in 2017.]

I served as the UPS VBRG President for two years and stepped down to focus my efforts on VETLANTA and to give another UPSer the opportunity to lead. I've continually stayed engaged with veterans affairs at UPS, working special projects and assignments over the years with HR, Corporate Communications, and the UPS Foundation including serving at the Chair of the UPS Veterans Council and standing up the first UPS Veterans Management Training Program in a partnership with the US Chamber Foundation Hiring our Heroes program.

The Joint Base Lewis McChord team hosting a C-17 Globemaster tour during our initial visit to stand up the first UPS Veterans Management Training Program

In 2017, I was selected as a finalist for the Jim Casey Community Service Award. This award, which was established in 1995, is the highest honor presented by UPS and is named after UPS's founder. Winners are chosen annually from individuals nominated by UPS's global work force of more than 500,000 employees with finalists being selected from the nominations and a winner chosen by a panel of UPS employees, UPS retirees, and community leaders. The Casey Award recognizes outstanding community service, a hallmark of UPS's corporate legacy and commitment to social responsibility.

This award is super prestigious and seeing the winner's story every year just blew me away and greatly inspired me. I didn't believe in a million years I would ever win it as the winners' stories and commitments to their communities are just unapparelled. I was nominated in 2016 and didn't make it as a finalist. I was nominated again in 2017 by co-worker and friend Terry Murray and we spent many hours together working on the awards package. I was in Hong Kong on a seven-week deployment for UPS during peak season in 2017 when I received the word in November that I was again a finalist. In January, I was invited to a secret meeting at my office and was informed that I had won the award. I was speechless. The kicker is the award is announced at the UPS Management Conference each year, which was still two months away, so I had to keep it a secret until then. I was able to tell my direct boss and my wife. Several UPSers who were in the Casey Award video also figured out that I had won but were sworn to secrecy.

In the next two months, UPS produced the award video, and I wrote a speech and practiced it no less than 750 times. I wanted to use the opportunity to inspire people and highlight that our military veteran employees are super capable and we hire veterans not out of charity, we hire them because they give UPS a competitive advantage. I didn't want to use a podium or a teleprompter and put way too much pressure on myself. If I could do it over again, I'd probably lighten up and enjoy it more. The UPS Management Conference is held in the second quarter each year and the top 150+ leaders in the company attend the three days of meetings and events. The meeting is normally in Atlanta, but in 2018 they decided to hold it in Toronto, Canada. I was to be the second to the last guest speaker with Prime Minister Justin Trudeau closing it out behind me.

One of the best things about the meeting was I got to bring Suzan with me, and this was so important since she had been my biggest cheerleader, a huge advocate of VETLANTA, and had sacrificed having me away for hundreds and hundreds of hours each year. We flew to Toronto on the evening of the second day of the conference but had a couple of events on the first day in Atlanta. I got to have lunch with the Casey Award judges and,

153

since it is blind judging, they didn't know who had been selected until I walked in the room. Many of the judges told me that I was a runaway winner that year and the judging hadn't been close, which just blew me away. That evening, Suzan and I had dinner with some of my leadership and leaders from the UPS Foundation which oversees the Casey Award.

After the lunch, I attended a meeting in the corporate compliance department and the head of our government compliance team, who is an Army veteran, graciously announced to the participants in the room and on the call that I was a Casey Award finalist. The funny thing is I mentioned that I'm keeping my fingers crossed and he informed me in a very blunt manner that it was clear that I hadn't won since the management conference had already started. I bit my lip and didn't say anything. After I got off the stage from accepting the award in Toronto, the very first text message I received was from him and he said, "Wow, I guess I was wrong" and wished me congratulations. It's a funny story and a great UPS memory.

In Canada, UPS put Suzan and I up in a different hotel than the conference participants as they closely guarded my identity until I'd walk on stage. They did sneak us into the conference center so I could practice the acceptance speech and we saw the Casey Award Video for the first time along with UPS Foundation President, Ed Martinez. Watching this video even today occasionally brings a tear to my eye, and on this evening I cried like a baby sitting between Suzan and Ed. It was very emotional seeing so many people that I think highly of, saying these incredible things about me and I had to excuse myself from the auditorium for five minutes while I composed myself. The only thing I was very disappointed about was they didn't include Suzan in the video. They had taped her but didn't include her in the final version. This hurt her feelings, but she sucked it up and she didn't want to dim the luster of the occasion. If I could do it all over again, I would have planned something very special for the next week to thank her. Despite this, we ended up having a phenomenal time in Canada and the trip was 1,000 times better since she was by my side.

I was so hyped up the night before the presentation that I didn't sleep one minute and practiced the speech another thirty times in the shower that morning. I was very nervous that I would fall apart emotionally during the video. Prior to being announced, I turned my back to the Casey video and played music into my earbuds. I was announced to a thunderous applause and absolutely nailed the speech. It was also nice to have Chris Peck in the audience as he was a VETLANTA Executive Advisor who'd been there from near the beginning and was my mentor.

Chris Peck and I in Toronto at the Management Conference in 2018

Over the course of the next two months, I was really treated like a rock star and would get introduced and get standing ovations at the UPS offices I visited. Then, as quickly as it came, it went and the adage of "what have you done for me lately" was back in play at UPS.

I'm so grateful for UPS as the company changed my life. I was able to start my second career, do amazing things for veterans, pay off my house, save for retirement, and support the US military around the globe through our contracts, but it didn't come without a cost. If there is anything that UPS knows how to do it is work and they work you hard and long, rinse and repeat. The stress at times is immense and there is always a lot of pressure to grow revenue and profitability each year despite market conditions.

They had also given me a huge, diverse responsibility and near the end of my time as a director, I had the responsibility which at one point and time was previously done by three directors. That was just the reality of the situation and, I'm not complaining, but it was tough and at times I was not always treated fairly. I ended up taking a senior manager position where I have real work-life balance now. More disappointing, at UPS is we lost most of our momentum in the veteran space. Chris Peck was the biggest advocate of veteran engagement in the company and as an HR Vice President was able to make real strides with our engagement. Chris retired and we also had our veteran advocate in Public Affairs retire and our Veteran Affairs Manager retired as well and was not replaced. Our momentum completely stalled to the point that it will take real efforts, real passion, real commitment, and meaningful investment just to get back to where we were.

One of the things that really hurt me with UPS was the lack of engagement from some after Suzan passed. One of my leaders, who I had known for many years and had a solid relationship with, didn't engage with me. He didn't show up for Suzan's Celebration of Life, didn't check on me even one time or even mention her passing. It was very disappointing, but I did have several co-workers who showed real compassion and the company did right by me by offering me plenty of time to get my life back in order. When you go through a tragedy like this, you really find out the character of people and who are your true friends and who have just been paying you lip service. I am so grateful that my VETLANTA family was there and stepped in to ensure I was okay. This journey has motivated me to ensure VETLANTA grows and thrives to ensure the community is in place to help a veteran or family member that is facing tragedy.

11
MY FAITH JOURNEY

"Be strong and take heart, all who hope in the Lord." "Give thanks to the Lord for He is good: His love endures forever." "For the Lord takes delight in His people; He crowns the humble and salvation." "God promises to make something good out of the storms that bring devastation to your life. (Romans 8:28)

September 28, 2021, is a day that will live in infamy for me. It was the worst day of my life but a day that justified all the time and effort I'd put into building the VETLANTA community as it was this community who came to my aid. After Suzan was removed from life support, Brandon and I immediately left the room as Suzan would want us to remember her alive. Brandon headed home to mourn, and I stayed as I was too weak and stunned to even walk out of the hospital. Seventy-two hours prior to this, we were spending our last day in Puerto Rico sightseeing, enjoying the weather, buying souvenirs, and Suzan as always was out seeking out stray cats to feed them. After we came home, she became ill, and all her organs shut down and the life drained out of her just so astoundingly quickly. This only happens on the medical shows she loved to watch on television or read about and now those shows and books had become her fate and my reality.

Within minutes of stepping out of the ICU, my phone started ringing and the first call was from Melissa Phillips, John's wife. She wanted to let me know that she, John, and a whole lot of others were praying for me, Suzan, and the boys and she wanted to know what she else could do to help. I didn't want Suzan to spend the night in the morgue, but I could barely even breathe let alone start coordinating arrangements. Melissa jumped into action, asked me a series of questions, and executed a plan of action with military precision. She took full responsibility of the early administrative requirements and arranged transportation, cremation, death certificate, and even brought Suzan's ashes to my home as I couldn't find the strength to hold the box with her ashes. She worked through the red tape and bureaucracy and kept me informed of her progress.

More importantly, sixteen months later, Melissa is still sending me these amazing emails even which relate good memories, dreams, and share the love and hurt. I was very surprised to find out that many people will avoid talking about a lost loved one, so they don't stir up the pain, but at times I needed to be reminded that others love and miss her as well. Melissa also told a story to me about a discussion she and Suzan had several years before she passed. Suzan had decided to stop working about a decade ago and really threw her efforts into establishing an amazing home for us and working on our relationship. Melissa asked her about what she was going to do in the future to be fulfilled and Suzan's answer was she was completely fulfilled and our life together was so amazing that she often must pinch herself to ensure she's not dreaming. This story is huge for me as I was always asking myself if I did enough to make her happy, did I tell her I love her enough, and did I treat her well enough. Hearing these words have comforted me so much.

My VETLANTA family stepped up in a big way and used the familiar VETLANTA routine to help me over the next several months starting with breakfast meetings just two days after Suzan passed. Instead of discussing strategy, planning the next summit, or vetting a nonprofit, my health and wellness became the sole agenda item, and these breakfasts would eventually turn into planning meetings for Suzan's celebration of life. They would take me to The Original Pancake House in Alpharetta sometimes three times a week for coffee, pancakes, and crispy bacon but also to ensure I was okay, listen, supply hugs, advice, and inspiration. These meetings were more important that Chris, Kevin, John, Patrick, Amy, Zack, Krista, and Stephanie will ever know. The entire VETLANTA Board planned Suzan's celebration event and executed it remarkably.

On October 30, 2021, we had 200+ VETLANTA members, co-workers, family members, neighbors, and friends show up to celebrate Suzan, and she would have been pleased as it looked more like a VETLANTA Summit than a funeral or wake. We had VETLANTA volunteers at the front welcoming people. Chris Peck served as master of ceremony. Kevin provided the prayer. Melissa, Krista, and my sister Joann told wonderful stories about Suzan. We had an amazing musician from the University of Georgia sing the National Anthem along with her favorite song, "Somewhere Over the Rainbow." The crowd spent an hour telling Suzan stories while looking at the 125 framed pictures around the room, which highlighted our adventures together. Brandon closed out the ceremony by speaking from the heart, and he surprised everyone with his courage and presence. We also had the three children of Rusty and Kelly Brown lead the Pledge of Allegiance. Suzan babysat Rusty for eight years at Wright-Patterson Air Force Base and at Edwards Air Force Base and they'd traveled all the way from Houston to attend. My friend the Tennesyrian traveled from

Los Angles and my roommate at Wright-Patterson, Phil, and his wife Amy made the trip from Ohio.

Somewhere over the rainbow

After the celebration of life, I had to face the reality of living without Suzan physically by my side, which I had not done since November 1986. I had to figure out what was best for me, what I liked to eat, how I wanted to live my life going forward, and figure out what would make me happy. I first started with mending my relationship with James and his new bride Meghan as we had been separated for a time and I'm blessed to have them in my life again along with my grandson Hudson. Spending time with Hudson was a mixed blessing at first because, while it was amazing, I always got emotional afterwards as it was so painful that Suzan was missing out on being a grandmother which was something she'd so looked forward to. I would be wrecked emotionally for hours after visiting with Hudson, but time has helped and God has given me the strength not only to endure but to be joyous in the occasion. I also got to see Brandon launch out of the house, which was good, but living by myself took some getting used to.

The days immediately following Suzan's death were rough. I had panic attacks and could barely sleep at night and my eating habits ranged from 400 calories a day to 4,000. I had Post Traumatic Stress Disorder (PTSD) from watching Suzan pass away after life support was removed and from seeing all those tubes and lines connected to her. During my time at VETLANTA, I had visited the SHARE Program at the Sheppard center which provides rehabilitation and care to military members with traumatic brain injuries, and they had routinely talked about the results they were seeing with patients with PTSD with Yoga therapy, so I decided to give it a try. I found a great local studio and the first class was the basics, which included box breathing. The breathing techniques would help mitigate the panic attacks and the hour during each class was a time which I had to pay attention and my mind wouldn't drift. The workouts quieted my mind, which is one of the goals of Yoga, and I eventually got into better shape mentally, physically, and spiritually.

One of the biggest changes was with my friendships. I have always had friends, but I never much needed them as my best friend had been by my side through thick and thin since I was seventeen. I quickly realized I needed friends and I needed to work on those relationships. This includes my friend Roger Roley. Roger is a retired Army Command Sergeant Major and a former tanker with two Purple Hearts. Roger started the FourBlock chapter in Atlanta and is now their regional manager for the southeast. FourBlock is an excellent nonprofit which provides transition assistance for veterans who left the military to pursue a college degree and now are getting ready to transition into the workforce and require transition assistance. Roger started the chapter around the same time VETLANTA was founded. We've partnered together over the years, and I volunteer routinely with them. Roger stepped up in a big way after Suzan passed and we started meeting routinely for lunch. Sadly, Roger's wife would pass away several months later after a long illness and I was able to return the favor and even help Roger with his faith journey. Before Suzan passed away, I would have never told anyone other than family members that I love them and now I value these friendships and have made this a routine occurrence.

Melissa helped me find a church and connect more closely with my faith. Suzan and I had always been believers and had solid faith but we had stopped going to church early on in our marriage after bad experiences with unsavory parishioners. I was very blessed as I had not lost my faith as some do after the loss of a loved one and my faith even got stronger. I started praying every day and became acutely aware of the blessings I did have. Melissa would ask me every week if I wanted to come to church but I wasn't quite ready for that step. Several weeks after Suzan passed, I received a very unexpected gift from Amy Stevens as she sent me a daily devotional, which is something that I had never seen but it at once became part of my routine. My good friend and fellow UPSer Terry Murray also encouraged me to find a church, and we spent many hours over the months talking about faith and my journey.

Kevin Horgan also started inviting me to attend his church and supplied excellent reading material, but the biggest push came from Lisa, the wife of my friend and VETLANTA Executive Advisor Chris Peck. Lisa, Chris, Suzan, and I would occasionally go out to eat and we loved spending time together and this continues today even without Suzan. During the first dinner together after Suzan passed, Lisa would not let me leave the restaurant until I agreed to join the small men's group that Chris leads with Northpoint Buckhead Church. I started attending the virtual meetings and became hooked as the fellowship became an important part of my healing process. I also no longer had an excuse to not attend church and agreed to go to church with John and Melissa.

Have you ever seen a job announcement and thought *They wrote this specifically for me?* That was my experience with attending GracePoint Church. This is a new church which came to existence in 2018 on Easter Sunday and the founders sum up the planting of this church.

> "What started as a dream and an opportunity by First Baptist Church of Alpharetta, GracePoint was strategically planted just inside southeast Cherokee County in the pathway of rapid new growth from Alpharetta, Milton, Hickory Flat, and Canton. In only a few short years, GracePoint has become a healthy, growing, independent church. Our church believes that life is an on-going process of growth, through successes and failures, good times and bad. We can either go about this process alone or we can connect with God and others in the church for friendship, support, and

wisdom. The truth is, doing life alone is lonely and difficult because we weren't created to be alone. Life is more joyful, meaningful, and fulfilling when we make a decision to grow with God."

GracePoint is a small church that provides an intimate connection with Pastor Chris and fellow worshippers, and they made me feel so welcome and so blessed. Every Sunday when I attend service or on the Wednesday evenings that I attend small group has made it so clear that a church is not a building, a church is the people that love God and love others, and I'm so blessed to have this church and to have key people in my life that guided my faith journey. According to its mission statement, GracePoint has a four-fold process to help us grow to be the persons God created us to be. We want to Connect (with God through his Son Jesus Christ and with others in the church), to Grow (to mature spiritually and in character), to Serve (pouring out to others the grace and goodness God is pouring into us), and to Share (telling the story of how God is transforming our life and has the power to transform others). The ultimate goal in this process comes from Romans 8:29, which tells us that from the very beginning God purposed us to become like his Son Jesus. We can't become more like Jesus on our own. Only through God's Spirit and allowing God to use others in our lives can we become who God has created us to be.

I don't have many regrets in my life, but I do regret not advancing my faith journey while Suzan was alive. She would have loved GracePoint and would have been very active. My faith journey is still in its early stages, but I'm thrilled to be thriving and helping others with their faith journey today. I've added the Veterans in Faith program to VETLANTA, which is something I had resisted in the past and now I'm convinced this will be our fastest growing offering going forward. I'm involved with several small groups, have attended services at several other churches, and will be attending Heroes Return, my first religious retreat.

Heroes Return is a four-day journey in beginning a walk seeking the Father's heart without distraction. The days provide the time needed for searching and listening to what the Father says is true about us. You will leave with a new identity as a son or daughter of our Heavenly Father, Abba, Pappa. . . . When we agree with God and walk into our identity we will begin to walk and lead in freedom. Participants of the Return and Reflect leave all distractions behind during these encounters. The greatest thing anyone can do for his or her family is become the man or woman God created them to be.

I'm often told that I'm doing so well with the grieving process, and I'm continually asked for advice. Sometimes I want to scream when I'm told this because the pain is real and is with me each and every day with different intensities; however, I know that I'm blessed as God has given me strength I never thought I had and he's put me on a path to help others, so here is my Top 10 pieces of advice.

1. God loves you, so take time to work on that relationship. Pray!

2. Treat your relationships like this is your last day together as it could very well be. Take time to tell your loved ones that you love them, give your spouse a hug and a kiss, and buy them flowers.

3. Take pictures together. I wasn't big on having my picture taken for many years but thankfully I changed and the pictures I have with Suzan are now my most treasured possessions.

4. If you have the resources, don't put off those bucket list items as the right time to do them is now.

5. Have those difficult conversations on what needs to be done after one of you passes away. Make sure you have an exact plan for cremation or burial.

6. The administrative burden was tough which included everything from not knowing the Netflix password to processing life insurance, changing names on titles and accounts. Make sure you both fully understand and know all the pertinent information like accounts, passwords, and combinations. Complete those Powers of Attorney, wills, living wills, and trusts now.

7. Fix what's broken.

8. Understand that it's okay to grieve and speak about your feelings and to seek help.

9. Understand there is no timetable in the grieving process nor a standard on how to grieve and each person's process is very different.

10. Surround yourself with an amazing community.

12
TILL WE MEET AGAIN

So, that's *Knight Work* and my journey to VETLANTA to this point. I consider the work to be completely unfinished, and I pray that God has important plans for me on earth so I can continue to make a difference to the point that my journey turns into a series of books. As I write these final words, I've just returned from Grand Cayman where I'd spread Suzan's ashes into the Caribbean Sea on a beach where we made so many beautiful memories. It was a very special day for me as it was the right place and the right time. It hurt deeply making the trip when I saw the excited couples and families at the airport as it reinforced my loss, but once I made it to the beach, God provided a beautiful moment of tranquility. I prayed and said parting words and afterwards God provided a peace that I had not felt in a very long time, and it felt as though a boulder had been lifted off my chest. I miss Suzan every day and, while the pain never leaves, I'm carrying on and committed to honoring her memory through my service to veterans and their families and I know I'll see her again in heaven.

See you again in heaven

DEDICATION AND ACKNOWLEDGEMENTS

This book is dedicated to the memory of Suzan. She had a greater impact than she would ever know and is loved and missed by many.

This book is for Hudson Knight. While you never knew your grandmother Suzan, my hope is when you read this book when you get older that you understand how amazing she was and know that she would have loved and cherished you.

Thank you to Sara Marshall and Terry Murray for encouraging me to write my story and to Kevin Horgan for the constant encouragement and for coaching and guiding me through the process.

My journey includes hundreds of friends, family members, co-workers, mentors, and VETLANTA members who have had an impact on my life and helped me with the VETLANTA journey, and while I can't mention everyone in this book, I want to say thank you to you all.